To Jennie,
Thank you for
precious daughter in Christ. Jennie
is a joy and source of inspiration for
this book. Be proud mom!
Blessings,
Ellen

BEAUTIFUL BALANCE

ELLEN BYHAM

Urban Press
P.O. Box 8881
Pittsburgh, PA 15221-0881 USA
412.646.2780
www.urbanpress.us

Beautiful Balance is dedicated to
my family and friends who have struggled
with anxiety and depression.
Join me on a journey to find balance...

 BEAUTIFUL BALANCE

Finding purpose in
God's two greatest
commandments.

"The most important one,"
answered Jesus,
"is this:
'Hear, O Israel:
The Lord our God,
the Lord is one.
Love the Lord your God
with all your heart and
with all your soul and
with all your mind
and with all your strength.'
The second is this:
'Love your neighbor as yourself.'
There is no commandment
greater than these."
Mark 12:29-31 NIV

Written by
Ellen Byham

Graphic Design by
Regina Johnson

Table of Contents

Preface

The purpose of this book is to express my desire to help women, and anyone else who reads it, gain some balance in their lives. We constantly strive to gain more. We constantly weigh ourselves in a set of balance scales that are not realistic. We can feel that we are always coming up short and that the scales are not tipped in our favor. I believe that every moment of our lives can be perfectly balanced if Jesus Christ is the focal point or fulcrum of the scales we so precariously set up for ourselves.

I will try and express some reasons for our crazy desires to be tipping the scales in our favor. I will also express my view that balance can be found with Jesus Christ. When you take the time to cultivate a relationship with Jesus Christ, you will discover a simple truth, that Jesus offers you the ability to be balanced. That balance is not always obvious but needs a bit of discovery on your part. The balance you are seeking also needs a bit of humility on your part. You must be humble enough to recognize that a greater power is the only way you will find balance.

I hope you enjoy the beautiful balance journey. Regina and I have enjoyed the discovery of this truth found in God's word for a couple years now, leading women's Bible study together. Beautiful balance is attainable. Enjoy reaching balance in your own life!

ᵏᵏᵏᵏ Introduction ᵏᵏᵏᵏ

To get started, I need to let you know where our beautiful balance journey begins. The balance I began to see in my own life started with an understanding of Jesus' words in Mark 12:29-31.

"The most important one," answered Jesus, "is this: 'Hear, O Israel: The Lord our God, the Lord is one. Love the Lord your God with all your heart and with all your soul and with all your mind and with all your strength.' The second is this: 'Love your neighbor as yourself.' There is no commandment greater than these."

When Jesus quotes these two greatest commands, he is being questioned by one of the teachers of the law, in his day. Every time these challenges came from the teachers of the law, they were hoping to trip Jesus up. Jesus always answered perfectly, using the word of God to teach those around him. Our balance comes from a relationship with Jesus which grows each time we read his word. The more time we spend in God's word, the more our relationship grows.

Loving God is the beginning of balance. Loving others is the continuation of the journey. Jesus' command sounds so simple, but we can make a real mess out of this. These two commands can be a filter for all the other scripture we read in the Bible. Every story told by Jesus, the law, the prophets and the Psalms and even the entire New Testament can be filtered back through these two commands. I have only just begun to touch the tip of the iceberg in studying God's word by filtering it all through these two commandments. I am happy to share some of the beautiful balance insights I have gleaned.

I will take you on a journey to learn what loving God and

loving others looks like. We will take some time to discover what it means to love God with your heart and soul, your whole mind and all your strength. We will also discover some truths together on the topic of loving others. Regina will balance me with her additional insights and fun artwork that she pieced together for great visuals. Enjoy our thoughts and visuals as you journey to find balance.

Jesus sits at the center of our balance. He is depicted by the cross at the bottom center of Regina's art work. The work Jesus did on the cross to restore humanity to once again have relationship with God is the basis for all balance for our lives. We will explore this beautiful balance in the chapter on heart and soul. Jesus knew how to love God with his whole being. Yes, I know that Jesus was God and that it appeared easy for him to love God like the scriptures commanded. But remember that Jesus was human also, and in his humanity, he struggled with all the emotions, and pain and suffering that we feel. He spent his life on earth leaving his legacy of loving God and loving others. Jesus was perfectly balanced in his heart, soul, mind and strength and he loved others with an awesome spiritual love that only comes through a loving relationship with God.

HEART AND SOUL This is our favorite visual, depicting the Cross of Christ which gives us the victory to be balanced, located in the center of our hearts, our true soul. Christ gives us new life that can be balanced in him. In this chapter, we will explore what a relationship with Christ is like. We will also explore love. What is love? How did God intend love for us? And how do you really love God in return? This is our spiritual center and the reality of loving God is based here. All the rest of the balance of each part of loving God with our whole being is found in our heart and soul.

MIND With this visual we need to remember that the brain is the physical house for our minds. Every thought is subject to God. Our understanding of love begins here for many people.

 The mind is the powerhouse of knowledge and understanding. With our mind we begin to understand who God is and what his intentions are toward us. It is with our minds that we make the rational decision to love God. Our hearts may already have moved toward God, but our minds make the final push toward exploring relationship with God and love. Many today are struggling with issues of the mind: anxiety, depression and other mental health related issues. I will take some time in this chapter to discuss some of these issues and what the Bible has to say about getting our minds healthy. We assume if we are capable of rational thought that all is well with our minds, but that might not be the case. Balancing our minds with Christ and his guidance will give us a beautiful perspective on life.

STRENGTH Our bodies are the source of physical strength for us and the house for our minds, and souls. A very important part of the whole picture of balance that God intended. Strength, when spoken of in the Bible has the meaning of physical

 power and bodily strength. As women, I know this means we are not as physically strong as our male counterparts, but we truly have capacity for physical strength. This is a tough topic for women and we struggle with our bodies. We will take some time to explore our physical bodies and what God intends for us as women. This is an area that is often out of balance for women. Western culture and the media often plague us with unrealistic views of our physical bodies. God has good news for us in his word and we will find some solid answers to battle any unbalance.

OTHERS Loving others completes the command that Jesus gave. That it how we put into practice what we are learning about loving God. Each person is made in the image of God

and we love God even more through loving others the way he intended for us. This is the Golden Rule that a good portion of the world has a bit of understanding about. Loving your neighbor as you would yourself is not an easy thing to accomplish. When your spiritual life is gaining some balance with a relationship with Christ and understanding how to go about loving God, the change in your spiritual life will make it possible to love others as Jesus preached about. Our time of exploring this topic will cover a lot of ground through the Bible. Most of our new testament focuses many teachings on expanding what Jesus meant for us in loving others.

So, this is how we will journey through Jesus' two greatest commands. We will explore our heart and soul, our minds, our physical bodies, and our relationships with others. I will walk you through a separate chapter for each topic to be discussed. We will thoroughly look at each part of us and how each part loves God and others and how each part must grow together toward being whole and being beautifully balanced.

CHAPTER TWO

✦ Heart and Soul ✦
The Beginning

In the Bible, and in many cultures around the world, the soul or spirit is also associated with the heart. In the early days, the heart was thought to reside in the 'guts' because this is where funny feelings would arise. An example of this would be the typical butterflies in the stomach and other such feelings. Of course, we know today that the heart is an organ in the middle of our chests. Those spiritual type feelings the people of history associated with the heart were caused by what we now know as chemical reactions going on in our bodies. They don't come from our hearts, but from our brain chemistry that is changing our bodies during different situations. The spirit or soul was thought to reside at the heart or center of the guts, which is where our actual heart is located.

Spiritually speaking, I am not really sure where our soul or spirit resides in our bodies. It is our essence, the part of us that is made in the image of God and it can't be captured, measured or transferred to others as our science fiction movies like to portray. It is certainly not like what the people of old thought either. We are much more complex than they imagined, and science has added to our knowledge in these modern days about our bodies and our hearts. Science still cannot answer the tough questions of our spirits or souls.

We go all the way back to the creation story in the first three chapters of the book of Genesis in the Bible to get an idea of spirit or soul. God created the world and everything in it from nothing. He spoke it into existence. That, my friends, is spiritual. It originated in God's creative power and still goes on today.

Everything God created was good because the spiritual nature of God himself is good.

I love the part of the Garden story where God planted trees for Adam and Eve (Gen 2:7-9). Depending on the version of the Bible you read it might say, "God planted," "God put," "God caused to grow"- you get the idea. What I like most about verse 9 is that there were trees that were pleasing to the eye (beautiful) and trees that were good for food. What is beauty? What is pleasing to

the eye? If you ask any artist to describe or give a definition of beauty they will stumble around for a few minutes and ultimately blurt out the words 'spiritual' or 'soul'. Even my online dictionary on my smart phone says that beauty is something that exhibits high spiritual qualities. Funny we find this in a day and age in which many would like to deny our spiritual existence.

This is where the story of Beautiful Balance begins. The part of us that is spirit or soul desires to get back to that beautiful and perfectly balanced relationship that existed in the Garden.

The creation story also reminds us that God breathed the breath of life into Adam (Genesis 2:7). It was after this that Adam became a living being. I am not going to go into a huge scholarly discourse on the Greek words for 'breath', 'breath of life', or 'living being' here. I will mention in passing that the original Greek word is referring to 'spirit' or 'soul'. Why did the writers of the Bible want us to know this? Because God

is spirit, we are God's special creation, and we were granted the personal privilege of getting God's spirit breathed into us. No other living creature got this privilege, only mankind. So, we have a soul, a spirit.

This is where the story of Beautiful Balance begins. The part of us that is spirit or soul desires to get back to that beautiful and perfectly balanced relationship that existed in the Garden. God loved his creation. God spent time in the Garden with Adam and Eve. God still desires to spend time with us today and have a relationship with us. Because Adam and Eve disobeyed God, they lost that time of intimate relationship and privilege of being in the Garden. Sin came into the world and relationship with God has been unbalanced ever since.

The great part of this story is that God fixed the problem of sin by sending his son Jesus to do the repair work that we were not capable of doing. Jesus took the sacrifice for our sin and made the way back to a balanced relationship with God. He died on the cross and rose again to live in heaven with God. Jesus compels us to come and follow him and learn the balanced secrets of leaning on him and being once again in intimate relationship with God. (If you don't know the whole story of the Bible and don't have a Bible, read the Bible online on Bible Gateway. Look up the gospel of Matthew, Mark, Luke, or John and read the whole story of Jesus for yourself).

Now, Jesus sits as the center point of our balance. How do we find balance in Jesus? First and foremost, our lives become new and remade spiritually when we follow Jesus as Lord and savior. He came to offer new life and renewed relationship with God. When we step out in faith and believe that he is the son of God and that he can forgive our sins and restore a balanced relationship with God, the Holy Spirit of God will enter our lives and begin a radical spiritual renewal in our lives.

All the unbalance and emptiness that we have had will begin to change. These changes are only happening because someone has shared the good news about Jesus with you or you have discovered it yourself by reading the Bible. Once you are here, you are realizing that yes, Jesus is our balance and we learn about the balance by reading God's word, hearing it spoken to us, or learning to memorize for ourselves. Every bit of balance we need to learn from Jesus will be found in the Bible.

CHAPTER THREE

﹌ Heart and Soul ﹌
Our Emotional Center

The Good, The Bad, and The Ugly

The philosophers of old called the heart and soul the emotional seat or center of man. My phone dictionary says:

THE HEART is the center for emotion, sympathy, feeling. The essential inner core of a person.

THE SOUL is the principle of life of a human, feeling and thoughts.

Those butterfly feelings in the center of your chest/stomach area gave the philosophers this idea. The physical reaction you have to emotions is very real. The discoveries of science have revealed much about how emotions are linked to body and mind to release hormones that cause the 'butterfly' reaction in our stomach or chest. As you can see, we are always a total whole spirit, mind, body and they operate in conjunction with each other. When one becomes severely unbalanced, the others will then fall out of sync as well. We will discuss each area separately, but they are forever and intimately connected in the beautiful creation God made us to be.

So, what? I have some emotions coming to the surface in my gut, what of it? Those emotions can save your life, if for instance – when it comes to that good old fight or flight reaction. I am about to get run over by a car coming up on the curb, what to do? Run or jump out of the way or stand there and get run over. Emotions are given to us for purpose and one of those purposes is just to survive.

I believe God gave us an emotional center for much more

than just survival. Emotions give us the link to relationship that
God intended. We can begin to feel that there is a God out there
who exists. We feel love with God and with others. Every emotion
has been created by God and they can all be a benefit to us. Love
is the most wondrous. It can mold us, passing on other feelings of
safety, protection, peace, satisfaction. Learning to understand that
all emotions are created by God and have a place in our lives is a
good thing.

A lack of love or even hatred can put up negative emotions
in our life like fear, unworthiness, anxiety, or depression. Having
an unbalanced load of negative emotions in our lives can prevent a
relationship with God and therefore, can harm relationships with
others. Digging deep into the Bible and seeing what God has to
say about some of these emotions he created is a good place to
start in understanding how we might gain some balance.

Let's travel through some of the scriptures to get an idea
of what God is doing with this emotional center he created in us.
The book of Genesis is the beginning. We see that God created
man and woman in his own image (Genesis 1:27). God gave them
the breath of life (Genesis 2:7). There is a uniqueness here with
man's creation. "In God's image" and "with the breath of life" are
significant. No other part of creation received that intimate connection to God – only mankind. Relationship. God intended from
the beginning to be in relationship with us. With you. Mull that
over for a moment. Your mind must be connected here to see the
connection to the heart and soul – see it's never really separated,
maybe just a bit unbalanced at times. God walked and talked with
Adam and Eve (Genesis 2-3), his intimately created beings made
in his image and who walked around with his breath of life. He
put man in a beautiful garden, and that is significant. Beauty is
defined as delighting the senses or mind. Emotions were being
tweaked right from the get go. And from the beginning, God was
working in us the positive emotions that delighted, gave safety,
protection, and love.

But…mankind had to mess all that up. God gave the one
small instruction to his creation to leave the tree in the middle of
the garden alone and we just couldn't keep our hands to ourselves

(Genesis 2:16-17). Yes, ladies, Eve, our wonderful mother of all mankind, took the first bite and we have been blasted with knowledge of everything. The protection, delight and safety of that beautiful garden was stripped away and we became aware. Aware of what? Aware that we just attempted to circumvent God and put ourselves in his place. A load of negative emotions came with this awareness (Genesis 3:7). Fear, anxiety, separation. Adam and Eve tried to hide from God in the garden. They realized the beautiful relationship that God had with them would never be the same. Curses came (Genesis 14-19) and they brought the awareness of many more negative emotions like pain, enmity or hatred, passion, etc. God sent Adam and Eve from the beautiful, protected garden into the world at large to bear the great burden of knowledge that they had put a separation in the relationship with a God who loved them and had intended every good thing for their existence.

> *But…*
> *mankind had to*
> *mess all that up.*
> *God gave the one*
> *small instruction*
> *to his creation*
> *to leave the tree in*
> *the middle of the*
> *garden alone and*
> *we just couldn't*
> *keep our hands to*
> *ourselves*
> *(Genesis 2:16-17).*

Mankind took the negative emotions and ran amuck with them until the great flood. Murder, envy, strife and many more disastrous things were going on in Noah's day and God made a move to destroy the beautiful creation he started. The flood came and destroyed all the earth but Noah, his family and all the creatures in the ark (Genesis 6-8). When Noah got off that ark alive, he sacrificed in thanksgiving and praise to God. God

smelled that pleasing aroma and said, "Never again will I curse the ground because of humans, even though every inclination of the human heart is evil from childhood. And never again will I destroy all living creatures, as I have done." Genesis 8:21

Our heart inclination is to go toward negative emotions that separate us from God, that caused the destruction of the whole earth at one point and every beautiful creature God created. Evil. I don't like that label. Our hearts go toward evil. Yuck. You get it. We all know the names of many negative emotions: hate, anger, fear, depression, malice, anxiety. The Bible even makes some lists regarding such evil emotions that not only have a name but an action. If an action goes with it, then the physical body is part and parcel. We are one-spirit, mind, body. Man can have lewdness, uncleanness, and greediness (Ephesians 4:19 NKJV), adultery, fornication, uncleanness, idolatry, sorcery, hatred, contentions, jealousies, outbursts of wrath, selfish ambitions, dissensions, heresies, envy, murders, drunkenness, revelries, and the like…(Galatians 5:19 NKJV). A major unbalance with no spiritual grounding is a way to gain victory toward the relationship with God and positive emotions that give life and peace can result in some evil, ugly living.

There is good news. We have a way to get back to God. He did not leave us without a path. He told us way back in the Old Testament after the flood and when many more people populated the earth again and did some striving to have relationship with him: "If you seek the Lord your God, you will find him if you seek him with all your heart and with all your soul" (paraphrase Deuteronomy 4:29). All our emotional center is connected to God. It seeks him, it desires to have relationship with him. We want the connection. How is that going to happen if we messed things up so bad?

It took some time but the rift we created, God fixed. He came in the flesh, born of a virgin woman and was named Jesus (John 1 and Matthew 1). We will get on with that later. Let's continue to look at some heart/soul emotions in the Old Testament and continue with God's story about our amazing heart/soul creation. Before we get to Jesus, we see God bring His people together to begin this good work of arriving in the flesh.

God begins by calling Abraham up out of a world of evil bent on worshipping anything but God. Abraham responded, and God promised to come in the flesh and heal this rift (Genesis 15. God confirms again what he will do through Abraham's descendants (Genesis 17 and Genesis 22). God had a plan and purpose.

Even with all the evil and negative emotions run amuck, God was not about to abandon the beautiful creation of man. Many generations passed before God did arrive. In each generation, they struggled with heart/soul and connecting to God.

King David is perhaps one of the most beloved relatives of Abraham. Many people connect with his character because he was described as a man after God's own heart. In Acts 13:22, the Apostle Paul proclaims on one of his mission trips: "After removing Saul, he made David their king. **God** testified concerning him: 'I have found David son of Jesse, **a man after my own heart**; he will do everything I want him to do.'" David was a beloved king and a man full of God's own heart. Why do we love him so? Because David lived on the brink, full of all the emotions God created and he wrote about it in the Psalms. David's life is about the love of God and love of others. He lived relationship with God and others to the fullest. Making good choices, greater choices and darn right stupid choices where heart/soul emotions manifested itself with no connection to mind (we get some good ole self-control of these emotions of ours from our mind if you haven't figured that out).

We also love David so much because he is the human fore-father of Jesus. The Scriptures point to this one far off relative of David who will become the Messiah, Immanuel, God with us. When scriptures say the "son of David," it means this one, the most waited for Savior. **Matthew 1:1** says, "This is the genealogy of Jesus the Messiah the son of David, the son of Abraham:" And also, Luke 1:32 says, "He will be great and will be called the Son of the Most High. The Lord God will give him the throne of his father David." I will challenge you to read your Bible, not just at this point in my book, but from the start and all throughout. God has his good words recorded for our benefit. Make good use of it. David has a lot of words recorded about his emotion filled life. You can read about David in First and Second Samuel, First and Second Kings, and First and Second Chronicles. You can find references to his life in other books of the Bible such as Acts, Hebrews, and Matthew. And most wonderful for us, we can read a good portion of the book of Psalms that was written by David.

The Good

Right from the start, God had a plan for David. God knew David's heart was inclined toward Him and desired a relationship with Him. Long before he became a famous king, God called the prophet Samuel to choose this new leader. Samuel arrived at David's home and looked over each of his brothers. David was the youngest and wasn't even in the house, he was looking after his father's sheep.

Samuel thought the oldest or strongest, maybe, would be chosen. He said to God, "Surely the Lord's anointed stands here before the Lord." But the Lord said to Samuel, "Do not consider his appearance or his height for I have rejected him. The Lord does not look at the things people look at. People look at the outward appearance, but the Lord looks at the heart." (1 Samuel 16:6-7). Seven sons passed by Samuel and God rejected them all. David was the eighth and youngest son and God finally said to Samuel, "Rise and anoint him; this is the one" (1 Samuel 1:12). I like this part of the story because the youngest, most unlikely son was chosen.

This makes me realize that no matter how young, insignificant or unlikely I feel, God has something planned for me. My emotions connect. David was probably overwhelmed with emotion. The youngest son would not have held much expectation in that culture for receiving much of anything. How overwhelming to get visited by the most famous prophet in your land and be anointed with oil (a significant symbolic gesture of the culture) in front of your father and seven older brothers!

David's anointing signified that he was being set apart by God for God's use and mighty plan. The anointing was an outward gesture that God was about to fill this person with his Holy Spirit and power. And, yes, the anointing signified a future kingship was on the way. I cannot fathom the array of emotions in that tent. David's overwhelming feelings of gratitude, love of God, thanksgiving, maybe even feelings of inadequacy, fear of his family's reaction. What about the brother's reactions? Maybe some jealousy and envy. How about Dad? Fear from the current king, jealousy he wasn't chosen, who knows? So, what does this young kid, newly anointed with God's Holy Spirit do? He heads down the local battle field where the current king, King Saul, and all his brothers are located (1 Samuel 17). He goes on an errand for his father because he is still at home taking care of sheep. He goes as an obedient younger son and takes a delivery of supplies to the brothers in the army camp. Doesn't sound very exciting.

David gets there and does his father's bidding. He heads to the front lines to find his brothers and realizes there is something significant going on. Each day an enemy soldier named Goliath comes out and challenges a man to come forth from Israel's army (David's people) and fight him, alone, to settle this battle situation. Some of the men tell him what is going on and that if an Israelite man can defeat Goliath, King Saul will even give his daughter in marriage to the man.

David's oldest brother, Eliab shows his emotions. The scriptures tell us in 1 Samuel 17:28 "When Eliab, David's oldest brother, heard him speaking with the men, he burned with anger at him and asked, 'Why have you come down here? And with whom did you leave those few sheep in the wilderness? I know how conceited you are and how wicked your heart is; you came down only to watch the battle." Whew. Eliab is jealous, envious and burning with anger. We have all had the same feelings. They are ugly emotions and can cause a lot of damage.

David made good choices here and did not react to his brother's false accusations. He continued to gather information and went about his business doing what that earlier filling and anointing by the Holy Spirit would prompt. David would go and defeat this giant Goliath. Sure, sounds heroic! Well, it is heroic! God doesn't put these awesome stories in scripture for us to read and go 'ho hum'. We see David, a young boy, filled with God's anointed power go out and defeat a giant!

What are some heart/soul lessons here? God is always de-siring for us to be in relationship with him. God gives us the Holy Spirit to prompt, guide, protect and deliver on getting his good purposes accomplished. David was a willing vessel and kept that heart/soul emotional part of himself balanced with God's leading and protection. We can be used by God in the same way if we are willing to keep our balance in him. Babies need changing, papers need copied, phone calls need tackled – you have your own giants and they may look a lot different than Goliath! God knows your giants and your battles, and he is in it with you all the way! Keep it beautiful, keep it balanced.

The Bad and The Ugly

How about my beloved David when he isn't so balanced in his heart/soul relationship with God? You probably know the story I will choose. Yes, good ol' lies, deception, adultery, murder and death of a child. The Bible tells it all and it is a soap opera of the juiciest kind. David and the story of Bathsheba. You can read the story for yourself in the Bible, 2 Samuel 11 and 12.

David is king and is much older now. You would think some self-control would be more apportioned to him and he would be less of a crazy hot headed young man who had slayed a giant. He just happens to be hanging out on the rooftop, in the hot time of year, when all the fighting men have left to do war for his kingdom. Hmmm, he looks down and sees a beautiful lady taking a bath in one of the pools. Bad combo—older, powerful king, young, powerless lady.

David plain and simply loses emotional control and takes what he wants. See how quickly going out of balance also affects the second great commandment? David is not too concerned with loving his neighbor in the way God intended in the command. He sleeps with Bathsheba, who happens to be married to one of his officers. Let's make this a full-blown soap opera. Bathsheba gets pregnant from this liaison and everyone will know adultery was afoot because all the fighting men, including her husband are off at war. She tells David.

David tries to remedy his little faux pas by calling Bathsheba's husband back from the front to have a bit of R&R with his beautiful wife. Bathsheba's husband has no part of looking like a weak schmuck who needs to get in the sack with his wife while all his men are battling and possibly dying for the kingdom. David gives up the effort and has his lead general take Bathsheba's husband back to the front, in the thickest heat of battle to make sure he doesn't come back. Nice! This great man after God's own heart just condones the assignation of one of his officers by using the battlefront as the assassin. The intrigue is growing. Bathsheba and David know what is going on. David's general is now in cahoots and what about all the other royal household help? Bathsheba's husband dies at the front. David marries her after her time of mourning. Not sure how long that was but in the meantime, she is growing fat with child, not her husband's child, but David's illegitimate child. I like the marriage factor here as a touch of concern on David's part — as if that is going to make up for what is going on.

Favorite part of the story comes now. God sends his prophet Nathan to give David a little shake up and reminder that his balance has slipped. Nathan shares this sad little story about a rich man taking away the only perfect little ewe lamb from a poor man to prepare a feast for his guest. Yeah, rich guy takes little lamb to cook it for dinner for his guest. A little cruel, a little over the top with the power over the poor guy.

David is enraged and wants to see the rich guy die because he abused his power and had no pity! Funny how we only see things we want to sometimes. Nathan looks right at David and says, "You are the man!" (2 Samuel 12:7). Then Nathan goes on a little discourse about God and his personal words to David. David is reminded about how in his balanced and right relationship with God, God gave him everything — his life, his kingdom, his wives — everything. And what? It wasn't enough. David had to go and abuse it by taking what God had not given him.

God pronounces some harsh judgement for David's unbalance. Look here folks, we ourselves can be the biggest source of unbalance in our lives. Letting our emotions, our heart/soul center run amuck with no self-control, tossing God off as if He can't see or doesn't know what is going on. God always knows. You might not get visited by a prophet, but rest assured God will get your attention back on him. Consequences of sin, that unbalance way back in the garden of Eden can be ugly and will be a definite result of unrestrained choices! Nathan delivers some serious news about the future happenings in David's royal house and kingdom. They are going to be ugly. David will be embarrassed beyond belief publicly because he sinned in secret. And God will take the baby born of adultery away in death! Slammer! Tough consequences indeed!

Good news. David repents at the news flash from Nathan. "I have sinned against the Lord" he proclaims in 2 Samuel 12:13. Nathan gives David the best of news because his heart is willing to repent, "The Lord has taken away your sin. You are not going to die." And the worst of News is delivered, "But because by doing this you have made the enemies of the Lord show utter contempt, the son born to you will die." 2 Samuel 12:13-14. Consequences follow. David gets slammed. God takes the life of the baby boy born to Bathsheba. Wow! That is an attention getter.

Sometimes our consequences are just as ugly, I won't try and gloss it over. Out of control balance, lack of leaning on God can be horrible. I know right now many of you are doing a replay of some sin scenario from your life and feeling all those emotions from the situation. Stop here and take a deep breath. When God forgives our sins, it is forever, never to be used against us again. We can enter God's presence, we can find balance again, but it is always on his amazing power. You need it – the beautiful balance of God, because the consequences that well up all those emotions might be for a lifetime.

"**As far as the east is from the west**, so **far** has he removed our transgressions from us" (Psalm 103:12). Remember that forgiveness and removal of sins are based on your willingness to repent. Repent and then begin leaning on God for the balance you need daily.

God's power is available to those who are called by his name and come to him for mercy. The Holy Spirit imparted to David, slew a giant. The Holy Spirit imparted to you makes you God's forever child and you are now a giant slayer in your life. Slay the giant that is preventing you from keeping balance.

God is not the great judge in the sky watching the balance scale of your sin weigh you down to hell. God is so much more than that. Therefore, I want you to read your

Bible and find out about him. His love is so great and awesome. God's love set a path for your salvation before you were even born. That is good news.

God in this picture of balance is more like this: God holds our heart/soul, our emotional capability of relationship in the palm of his hand. We are tender and frail. God knows every detail of our created spirit, mind and body. God forgives, and God plans on using us. He has plans and purposes just like he did for King David.  David stayed on with God even through the sin consequences. This verse comforts me, "So do not fear, for I am with you; do not be dismayed, for I am your God. I will strengthen you and help you; I will uphold you with my **righteous right hand**." Isaiah 41:10. God is the balance. God brings the beautiful balance. God's love makes it happen.

The first chapter of Ephesians tells about this amazing love from God that is lavished upon us. We are not left powerless in the sins we have made. Nor do we have to live defeated in the consequences. We can lift our heads and live with purpose. Those purposes of God go back to the greatest two commandments. We find that loving God with our whole heart/soul, mind and body gives us purpose and we are then filled to love others. King David did it, we can too.

> [1]Paul, an apostle of Christ Jesus by the will of God, to God's holy people in Ephesus, the faithful in Christ Jesus: [2]Grace and peace to you from God our Father and the Lord Jesus Christ.
>
> [3]Praise be to the God and Father of our Lord Jesus Christ, who has blessed us in the heavenly realms with every spiritual blessing in Christ. [4]For he chose us in him before the creation of the world to be holy and blameless in his sight. In love [5]he predestined us for adoption to sonship through Jesus Christ, in accordance with his pleasure and will— [6]to the praise of his glorious grace, which he has freely given us in the

One he loves. [7]In him we have redemption through his blood, the **forgiveness of sins**, in accordance with the riches of God's grace [8]that he **lavished on us**. With all wisdom and understanding, [9]**he made known to us the mystery of his will according to his good pleasure, which he purposed in Christ,** [10]to be put into effect when the times reach their fulfillment—to bring unity to all things in heaven and on earth under Christ.

[11]**In him we were also chosen, having been predestined according to the plan of him who works out everything in conformity with the purpose of his will,** [12]in order that we, who were the first to put our hope in Christ, might be for the praise of his glory. [13]**And you also were included in Christ when you heard the message of truth, the gospel of your salvation. When you believed, you were marked in him with a seal, the promised Holy Spirit,** [14]**who is a deposit guaranteeing our inheritance until the redemption of those who are God's possession—to the praise of his glory** (Ephesians 1:1-14 author's bold).

Let's continue exploring some of David's emotions that he exposes in the Psalms he writes. Our emotional center is quite full. David captures emotional moments in scripture like no other. Not only does David write poetically, he is gifted by God to receive prophecies that reveal the Messiah to come, Jesus, Son of David, who saves the people from their sins.

Psalm 22: 14-21, a prophetic psalm about Jesus:

[14]I am poured out like water, and all my bones are out of joint. My heart has turned to wax; it has melted within me. [15]My mouth is dried up like a potsherd, and my tongue sticks to the roof of my mouth; you lay me in the dust of death. [16]Dogs surround me, a pack of villains encircles me; they pierce my hands and my feet. [17]All my bones are on display; people stare and gloat over me. [18]They divide my clothes among them and

cast lots for my garment. [19]But you, Lord, do not be far from me. You are my strength; come quickly to help me. [20]Deliver me from the sword, my precious life from the power of the dogs. [21]Rescue me from the mouth of the lions; save me from the horns of the wild oxen.

Psalm 32, a psalm about confession and forgiveness:

[1]Blessed is the one whose transgressions are forgiven, whose sins are covered. [2]Blessed is the one whose sin the Lord does not count against them and in whose spirit is no deceit. [3]When I kept silent, my bones wasted away through my groaning all day long. [4]For day and night your hand was heavy on me; my strength was sapped as in the heat of summer. [5]Then I acknowledged my sin to you and did not cover up my iniquity. I said, "I will confess my transgressions to the Lord." And you forgave the guilt of my sin. [6]Therefore let all the faithful pray to you while you may be found; surely the rising of the mighty waters will not reach them. [7]You are my hiding place; you will protect me from trouble and surround me with songs of deliverance. [8]I will instruct you and teach you in the way you should go; I will counsel you with my loving eye on you. [9]Do not be like the horse or the mule, which have no understanding but must be controlled by bit and bridle or they will not come to you. [10]Many are the woes of the wicked, but the Lord's unfailing love surrounds the one who trusts in him. [11]Rejoice in the Lord and be glad, you righteous; sing, all you who are upright in heart!

Psalm 91, a prophetic psalm of Jesus, a psalm many use for comfort and to pray protection over loved ones:

[1]Whoever dwells in the shelter of the Most High will rest in the shadow of the Almighty. [2]I will say of the Lord, "He is my refuge and my fortress, my God, in whom I trust." [3]Surely he will save you from the fowler's snare and from the deadly pestilence. [4]He will

cover you with his feathers, and under his wings you will find refuge; his faithfulness will be your shield and rampart. [5]You will not fear the terror of night, nor the arrow that flies by day, [6]nor the pestilence that stalks in the darkness, nor the plague that destroys at midday. [7]A thousand may fall at your side, ten thousand at your right hand, but it will not come near you. [8]You will only observe with your eyes and see the punishment of the wicked. [9]If you say, "The Lord is my refuge," and you make the Most High your dwelling, [10]no harm will overtake you, no disaster will come near your tent. [11]For he will command his angels concerning you to guard you in all your ways; [12]they will lift you up in their hands, so that you will not strike your foot against a stone. [13]You will tread on the lion and the cobra; you will trample the great lion and the serpent. [14]"Because he loves me," says the Lord, "I will rescue him; I will protect him, for he acknowledges my name. [15]He will call on me, and I will answer him; I will be with him in trouble, I will deliver him and honor him. [16]With long life I will satisfy him and show him my salvation."

Psalm 100, a psalm of praise and thanksgiving:

[1]Shout for joy to the Lord, all the earth. [2]Worship the Lord with gladness; come before him with joyful songs. [3]Know that the Lord is God. It is he who made us, and we are his; we are his people, the sheep of his pasture. [4]Enter his gates with thanksgiving and his courts with praise; give thanks to him and praise his name. [5]For the Lord is good and his love endures forever; his faithfulness continues through all generations.

Psalm 119, excerpts exposing affliction and consequences:

[71]It was good for me to be afflicted so that I might learn your decrees. [72]The law from your mouth is more precious to me than thousands of pieces of silver and gold. [73]Your hands made me and formed me; give me understanding to learn your commands. [74]May those

who fear you rejoice when they see me, for I have put my hope in your word. [75]I know, Lord, that your laws are righteous, and that in faithfulness you have afflicted me. [76]May your unfailing love be my comfort, according to your promise to your servant. [77]Let your compassion come to me that I may live, for your law is my delight.

Psalm 121, a psalm used during travel:

[1]I lift up my eyes to the mountains— where does my help come from? [2]My help comes from the Lord, the Maker of heaven and earth. [3]He will not let your foot slip—he who watches over you will not slumber; [4]indeed, he who watches over Israel will neither slumber nor sleep. [5]The Lord watches over you—the Lord is your shade at your right hand; [6]the sun will not harm you by day, nor the moon by night. [7]The Lord will keep you from all harm— he will watch over your life; [8]the Lord will watch over your coming and going both now and forevermore.

Psalm 145, a psalm of God's love and its benefits:

[1]I will exalt you, my God the King; I will praise your name for ever and ever. [2]Every day I will praise you and extol your name for ever and ever. [3]Great is the Lord and most worthy of praise; his greatness no one can fathom. [4]One generation commends your works to another; they tell of your mighty acts. [5]They speak of the glorious splendor of your majesty—and I will meditate on your wonderful works. [6]They tell of the power of your awesome works— and I will proclaim your great deeds. [7]They celebrate your abundant goodness and joyfully sing of your righteousness. [8]The Lord is gracious and compassionate, slow to anger and rich in love. [9]The Lord is good to all; he has compassion on all he has made. [10]All your works praise you, Lord; your faithful people extol you. [11]They tell of the glory of your kingdom and speak of your might, [12]so

that all people may know of your mighty acts and the glorious splendor of your kingdom. [13]Your kingdom is an everlasting kingdom, and your dominion endures through all generations. The Lord is trustworthy in all he promises and faithful in all he does. [14]The Lord upholds all who fall and lifts up all who are bowed down. [15]The eyes of all look to you, and you give them their food at the proper time. [16]You open your hand and satisfy the desires of every living thing. [17]The Lord is righteous in all his ways and faithful in all he does. [18]The Lord is near to all who call on him, to all who call on him in truth. [19]He fulfills the desires of those who fear him; he hears their cry and saves them. [20]The Lord watches over all who love him, but all the wicked he will destroy. [21]My mouth will speak in praise of the Lord. Let every creature praise his holy name for ever and ever.

David speaks of every emotion either directly or indirectly in his Psalms. This is what exposes him as such a favorite Bible character. David loves God and others. David hates sin in himself and others. David falls from grace, his life is being sought after, he conquered a kingdom, he commits adultery, he messes up raising his kids. You name it and David has felt it. David lived the good, the bad and the ugly of emotions. We live the good, the bad and the ugly of emotions every day. I believe that God gives us all this fantastic information regarding emotions in his word to keep us in Beautiful Balance.

Our emotions connect us inexplicably to a God who created us and our emotions. Paul sums up this idea of the center of emotion in Acts 17:28 'For in him we live and move and have our being.' As some of your own poets have said, 'We are his offspring.' God knows our every emotion. The core of the heart/soul is love. Because he loved us first and created us to know what love and relationship look like we can now love in return. We are capable of loving God and loving others. God is not just some spiritual concept in the sky floating about making us 'feel good' occasionally. God is spirit, very real and very present in our lives. The first commandment is to love God with our whole heart/soul, mind and strength. Love would exist if we did not, because love is God. It is God's love that created, it is God's love that binds a relationship with his creation. It is the relationship with God first that makes love the most amazing emotion to discover.

We love God with heart/soul first because that is the emotion center of our being. We love God with mind and body as well because we are perfectly and intimately created as a one package deal. The deal is that we come to God as whole being, heart/soul, mind, body. Emotions expose us and get going in the relationship, but the mind and body come along for the ride. Each will show us more about ourselves and this God who created the heart/soul, emotion center of our being. We will continue to discover more truths about God, the love he has for us and the balance we find in relationship with him.

Hope, the Expectant Emotion

Before we move on to the mind and body, I wanted to discuss the most wonderful emotion that makes the Christian life worth living. Hope. It is a small word that invokes much. I never really thought of hope as an emotion until I started on this book. I have been amazed to learn about every emotion a person has ever felt described in the scriptures. I have wondered at these emotions and been pleasantly pleased to discover love at the core, but hope as the connecting cord gently inviting us into relationship with God.

I asked a class of ladies to describe hope for me. It was a very hard concept to describe without launching into a personal story that depicted the essence of what they wanted to convey. The first answer blurted out was that hope is God. Nice. Very simplistic and probably the basic truth mankind needs to hear. The truth of the Bible is much simpler than some would believe. Other answers included: hope carries you through the hard times and hope is a yearning for something more than just yourself. The stories came out one by one. At the center was God, the very real relationship they have with God and the very real things he has given them hope about, to go on day to day in their Christian walk.

Hope is that little cord... that connects us to love. Hope can get a person moved on to the next day even when all looks lost.

I asked them if they had ever thought of hope as an emotion. No, they replied. But after serious consideration they agreed that hope is an emotion. God gives it and it is connected to his love. The Apostle Paul talks about faith, hope and love in 1 Corinthians 13. Love is the greatest, but hope and faith come in on the top three.

Hope is that little cord, like I said, that connects us to love. Hope can get a person moved on to the next day even when all looks lost. David, that lover of emotion and super psalm writer, has a wonderful psalm about hope.

Psalm 25

[1]In you, Lord my God,
I put my trust.
[2]I trust in you;
do not let me be put to shame,
nor let my enemies triumph over me.
[3]No one who hopes in you
will ever be put to shame,
but shame will come on those
who are treacherous without cause.
[4]Show me your ways, Lord,
teach me your paths.
[5]Guide me in your truth and teach me,
for you are God my Savior,
and my hope is in you all day long.
[6]Remember, Lord, your great mercy and love,
for they are from of old.
[7]Do not remember the sins of my youth
and my rebellious ways;
according to your love remember me,
for you, Lord, are good.
[8]Good and upright is the Lord;
therefore he instructs sinners in his ways.
[9]He guides the humble in what is right
and teaches them his way.
[10]All the ways of the Lord are loving and faithful

toward those who keep the demands of his covenant.
¹¹For the sake of your name, Lord,
forgive my iniquity, though it is great.
¹²Who, then, are those who fear the Lord?
He will instruct them in the ways they should choose.
¹³They will spend their days in prosperity,
and their descendants will inherit the land.
¹⁴The Lord confides in those who fear him;
he makes his covenant known to them.
¹⁵My eyes are ever on the Lord,
for only he will release my feet from the snare.
¹⁶Turn to me and be gracious to me,
for I am lonely and afflicted.
¹⁷Relieve the troubles of my heart
and free me from my anguish.
¹⁸Look on my affliction and my distress
and take away all my sins.
¹⁹See how numerous are my enemies
and how fiercely they hate me!
²⁰Guard my life and rescue me;
do not let me be put to shame,
for I take refuge in you.
²¹May integrity and uprightness protect me,
because my hope, Lord, is in you.
²²Deliver Israel, O God,
from all their troubles!

David lets his reader know right away that hope in the Lord is a sure thing. Hope keeps a person, guides a person and brings a person right into the loving arms of God. Hope is an emotion that binds us to God's love. In this psalm, David tells us that hope gives us knowledge of God's ways, the sinner can be instructed, a relationship, a covenant can be made by God toward man with hope. God instructs, teaches, guides, gives

Hope:
The
Expectant
Emotion

grace, guards, rescues, forgives, delivers and keeps a person whose hope is set on God. I like this emotion!

How does God do this hope thing? Where do we find out about it? If we are supposed to be taught, instructed and guided where is all that information? David does a good job of letting us know that hope is found in the word of God, Psalm 119:114 says, "You are my refuge and shield; I have put my hope in your word." The entire work of Psalm 119 is very lengthy and goes about using hope in God's word as a consistent theme.

"Never take your word of truth from my mouth, for I have put my **hope in your laws**." Psalm 119:43

"May those who fear you rejoice when they see me, for I have put my **hope in your word**." Psalm 119:74

"My soul faints with longing for your salvation, but I have put my **hope in your word**." Psalm 119:81

"I rise before dawn and cry for help; I have put my **hope in your word**." Psalm 119:147

Hope is the word of God. In the word of God, we find everything we will ever need. The hope, the word, gives us salvation, relationship and love. Those things come because the word reveals the truth of God. Is the emotion center, the heart/soul of us, finding this out without using the mind to read it to us, or the body to hear it for us being preached? The whole of us take part in this fantastic hope. A Beautiful Balance—love with hope drawing us in!

This hope, this word of God has a name – **Jesus**.

"The word became flesh and made his dwelling among us. We have seen his glory, the glory of the one and only Son, who came from the Father, full of grace and truth" (John 1:14).

God, the word, the hope, began revealing himself in creation even long before the words were written down in script by the prophets, kings, and apostles. No man is without excuse in the revelation of God and his desire to have relationship with us.

"For since the creation of the world God's invisible qualities—his eternal power and divine nature—have been clearly seen, being understood from what has been made, so that people are without excuse" (Romans 1:20).

God walked in the garden with Adam and Eve. His revelation was sure and true. His desire was to be in relationship with his creation, his people, the work of his hand. Hope draws us in like a sweet breath of mountain top air. God is in that breath. God who came in the flesh as Jesus Christ. Whatever for? To cement the hope of the heart/soul, relationship, strong and true and eternal. Love forevermore.

Job in his suffering wrote:

"Though he slay me, yet will **I hope in him**; I will surely defend my ways to his face." Job 13:15

David again in the Psalms writes of hope:

"But the eyes of the Lord are on those who fear **him**, on those whose **hope** is **in** his unfailing love." Psalm 33:18

"Why, my soul, are you downcast? Why so disturbed within me? Put your **hope in** God, for I will yet praise **him**, my Savior and my God." Psalm 42:5

"Yes, my soul, find rest in God; my **hope** comes from him." Psalm 62:5

Jesus, God in the flesh, is the hope of all mankind. The prophets wrote of hope in God often and many verses were about this Messiah, this Jesus who would come. When Jesus was busy doing ministry and miracles, Matthew wrote, "In his name the nations will put their hope." Matthew 12:21 quoting the prophet Isaiah 42:1-4.

Paul reminds the new followers of Jesus of his origin and that God fulfilled a promise of **hope** to Abraham, "Against all **hope**, Abraham in hope believed and so became the father of many nations, just as it had been said to him, "So shall your offspring be." Romans 4:18 Abraham never saw this hope, but believed and we benefit from that hope long ago. Paul also quotes the prophet Isaiah 11:10 "And again, Isaiah says,

"The Root of Jesse will spring up, one who will arise to rule over the nations; in him the Gentiles will hope." Romans 15:12 We are those far off relatives of Abraham, we are those

Gentiles who can meet the hope of God, here and now.

What are some benefits of this hope emotion and knowing Jesus?

> "May the God of **hope** fill you with all joy and peace as you trust in him, so that you may overflow with **hope** by the power of the Holy Spirit." Romans 5:13

> "It always protects, always trusts, always **hopes**, always perseveres." 1 Corinthians 13:7

> "He has delivered us from such a deadly peril, and he will deliver us again. On him we have set our **hope** that he will continue to deliver us," 2 Corinthians 1:10

> "For through the Spirit we eagerly await by faith the righteousness for which we **hope**." Galatians 5:5

> "I pray that the eyes of your heart may be enlightened in order that you may know the **hope** to which he has called you, the riches of his glorious inheritance in his holy people," Ephesians 1:18

> "There is one body and one Spirit, just as you were called to one **hope** when you were called;" Ephesians 4:4

> "The faith and love that spring from the **hope** stored up for you in heaven and about which you have already heard in the true message of the gospel." Colossians 1:5

> "That is why we labor and strive, because we have put our **hope** in the living God, who is the Savior of all people, and especially of those who believe." 1 Timothy 4:10

> "But Christ is faithful as the Son over God's house. And we are his house, if indeed we hold firmly to our confidence and the **hope** in which we glory." Hebrews 3:6

> "We have this **hope** as an anchor for the soul, firm and secure." Hebrews 6:19

> "Let us hold unswervingly to the **hope** we profess, for

he who promised is faithful." Hebrews 10:23

"Praise be to the God and Father of our Lord Jesus Christ! In his great mercy, he has given us new birth into a living **hope** through the resurrection of Jesus Christ from the dead," 1 Peter 1:3

"But in your hearts revere Christ as Lord. Always be prepared to give an answer to everyone who asks you to give the reason for the **hope** that you have. But do this with gentleness and respect," 1 Peter 3:15

The benefits of hope are a relationship with God through Jesus Christ, joy and peace, power in the Holy Spirit, faith, righteousness, security, firmness, and an eternal home as we are raised to life. We have a living hope and we will live eternally in this hope and hope calls out for you to seek, find, and follow Christ. The scriptures tell us that if you seek with your whole heart you will find. Jesus said, "**but seek first his kingdom and his righteousness, and all these things will be given to you as well.**" Matthew 6:13 God has not hidden himself, he reveals the path to know him clearly in the Bible. Let the God of hope guide you into an eternal relationship with him.

A Story of Hope

I wanted to add one of my favorite Bible stories of hope here. The story of Hannah is one that touches deeply in the heart/soul of a woman. Hannah's hope was surely in God; but her deep desire, that heart felt emotion, driving her day after day was to become a mother. Please read the story of Hannah in your Bible found in 1 Samuel 1-2:21. Enjoy my paraphrase:

Hannah was so concerned about being childless that it led her to pray a deeply spiritual cry in the worship center of her day. She was crying out to God in silence while moving her lips as if she were talking aloud. I do this a lot! The priest Eli, at the time, viewed this and accused her of being drunk in the house of God. Hannah was shocked and spilled out all her personal turmoil to Eli. Eli offered her compassion and asked God as well, to grant Hannah's prayer for a child.

I put this story here for a reason. Back to the present. Many, many friends I know have found themselves in the same spot as Hannah. The deep desire to become a mother looks no different today than it did thousands of years ago for Hannah. When it boils down to the nitty gritty, all the science and technology and newfangled ways of infertility treatment may not finish the deed. In the very depth of our heart/soul, we know that life is a gift from God and from God it will flow, science or not. The cries and prayers of my friends echo sweet Hannah.

God Almighty, giver of life, chose to bless Hannah with a child, a son, named Samuel. Samuel means, *God has heard*. An appropriate name for the new boy! I did not reveal the entire content of Hannah's heart felt prayer for a child. She offered the first-born child God would give her back to him. That is not a deal many women would offer up to God. They want that child but have no intention of giving it 'back to God'.

Hannah did it. She kept Samuel until he was weaned and took him, literally and physically, back to God. She took him right back to the house of worship and handed him to the priest Eli. Hannah's hope materialized before her eyes as her stomach grew for nine months and on the day of his birth, Samuel appeared. Beautiful, healthy, bouncing baby boy. Hannah's hope in God gave her a very real and physical baby boy. Amazing faith, to follow through with her human promise of giving the boy back.

> *Hope deferred makes the heart sick, but a longing fulfilled is a tree of life. Proverbs 13:12 (NIV).*

Hannah's hope was not in vain. The scriptures tell us, **"Hope deferred** makes the heart sick, but a longing fulfilled is a tree of life." Proverbs 13:12. Hannah lived the very essence of this proverb. She felt the sickness, the deep seated emotional loss and unresolved issue of being childless. She lived the glorious truth of her desire coming to life before her very eyes. God blessed

Hannah beyond that one child. Later, Hannah had more children by a gift of grace, three more sons and two daughters.

My heart breaks for those of you in Hannah's position. Keep leaning on the God of hope to gain your balance. He is the giver of life and he does intend good for those who are his children (Romans 8:28). Many of you need God's hope over a situation different than infertility. No matter, the God of hope is in your story of balance too. Nothing is too big to bring before a God of hope.

Lady M, a modern-day Hannah

Lady M also found herself in Hannah's situation. Childless, calling out to God to fulfill a desire to become a mother, and enjoy parenting and family life with her husband. Many prayers and many inquiries as to choices such as infertility treatment, fostering or adoption. Lady M and her husband went with the route of adoption. The process went smooth and the amazing result was a beautiful baby boy. Mothering fulfilled. Family life and parenting going full steam ahead. And several years later, what's this 'sick stomach' Lady M is feeling? Hmm, a glorious blessing by God, a miracle baby girl! An all-natural bonafide blessing of God, created the old-fashioned way between the love of a husband and wife! This God of hope is amazing and blesses exactly in the ways he intends to fulfill his good purposes in each life he has created.

Where is God taking the purposes and hopes of his two greatest commandments in your life? Beautiful Balance is God's greatest two commandments and believe me, he has got this!

My Story of Hope

My story is not quite like Hannah's. I was already a mom to five young children at the time of this story, approximately 18 years ago. My youngest at the time was about one. I was sitting at my kitchen table, in the quiet of the evening after putting five little wild children to bed. I just wanted five minutes to myself to do some devotions, reading God's word and praying before trying to connect to my hubby. I sat down with my cup of tea, my journal and my Bible and looked out the dark window into the nothingness.

I recollected a challenge I made to myself a few years back, as a new Christian. I needed some more love and expression of compassion in my life. I remembered a missionary who had been at our church speaking about orphans and the need to be the feet and hands of Jesus for these kids. I sat there thinking how wonderful it would be to adopt and add to our already big family. I don't even remember the scripture passage I was reading, because at that very moment I heard the voice of God say very clearly, "I have a daughter for you in India." Yep, the real audible voice of God that people say today you aren't supposed to hear. Well, I heard it loud and clear and looked around like a loony. No one was in the kitchen with me, not even our dogs.

For real God, this is not supposed to be happening. Okay, I am a woman of faith. If God wants to speak out loud so be it. I wrote it down and reflected. My first thought was, my husband is not going to believe this, and he is going to think I am nuts. I closed my journal and headed off to bed.

I handled it like a Christian pro. Called all my sisters-in-faith, the super close ones, the next day and asked for prayer. I told them, "I need you to pray that my husband will be receptive to a request to adopt another child. Fast and pray with me for the next two weeks and then I will make a petition to him." I wasn't taking any chances here girls. No little Esther fasting and prayer for only three days and nights. I drank water of course, but went without much food for the whole two weeks.

I called family services and set up an appointment to discuss adoption.

I thought this would be a good way to break the ice with hubby dearest. A dinner date and time alone away from the five little ones would follow. Two weeks of fasting to prepare this guy's heart to accept my words from God about adopting our newest little one from India!

Appointment day. My husband and I listened intently to information about foster care and local adoption. Out to our dinner date after. "Well," I asked my husband, "what do you think about adopting and adding to our family?"

"Look," he said, "I am all for adopting, I think it's the right Christian thing to do, but I am not up for foster care or trying a local adoption that most likely won't go through. It would kill you and the kids to have a baby taken away." Honest answer. It would kill me.

Hope has a name:
JESUS!

Here comes the two-week bomb blast I have been fasting and preparing for… "What would you say to adopting a little girl from India?" Speechless. That's a good sign. I thought for sure he would rant like a crazy man, in a controlled kind of way in that public and large restaurant. Yes, the dinner date was a premeditated safety zone for the bomb blast. Holding my breath now as the speechless manner continues. The stare down, eye to eye. Then the big smile and he says, "Out with it, what is it that you know?" He knows me so well.

I blurted it out. The whole audible voice of God stuff and everything. He reacted well. I cannot thank my sisters in Christ enough for their sacrifice and fasting and prayer over me the two weeks prior. "Who am I to argue with God?" my husband says, "If God is in this, then it will truly happen."

And my journey of hope deferred began. Miracle after miracle God performed an amazing process of adoption from India for our family. Three long years later, after delay and delay, added cost and miracle money, I arrived at the orphanage in India. My first thoughts on seeing our little girl, "What a wee little fairy baby!" My Irish mom would have been proud. She was a tiny and exquisitely beautiful little girl of two, just like a fairy in the stories my mom told me as a child. And life began anew for our family of six now! "Hope deferred makes the heart sick, but a longing fulfilled is a tree of life" (Proverbs 13:12).

Put your hope in the God of all hope. Hope has a name: JESUS!

CHAPTER FIVE

ᐊᐊᐳᐳ The Mind ᐊᐊᐳᐳ

The mind is our deeply joined and intimate powerhouse connected to our emotion center. The philosophers of old called the mind the seat of intellect. The dictionary describes the mind as the element, part or substance of a human that reasons, thinks, wills, perceives and judges. Our mind perceives the emotions we just discussed. Without a mind, there is no concept of any emotion one might be feeling. The connection is a perfect union.

The mind gives us understanding and knowledge that will help us reason, think and make a judgement concerning this God who wants to be in relationship with us. Our heart/soul may have been receptive and ready to be in relationship very quickly. But some are a tougher lot, and must use their mind to grasp what God has been working in their heart/ soul. It is a dynamic relationship and one cannot get along well without the other. Balance is needed.

> *Without a mind, there is no concept of any emotion one might be feeling. The connection is a perfect union.*

Old Testament on the Mind

What are some things the Old Testament scriptures reveal about the mind? God has a mind, Numbers 23:19

"God is not human, that he should lie, not a human being, that he should change his mind. Does he speak and then not act?

Does he promise and not fulfill?" God is steady in his mind." This is a relief, because then it secures the hope we want fulfilled in the promises that God recorded in the Bible.

King David said to his son,

> "And you, my son Solomon, acknowledge the God of your father, and serve him with wholehearted devotion and with a willing **mind**, for the Lord searches every heart and understands every desire and every thought. If you seek him, he will be found by you; but if you forsake him, he will reject you forever."
> 1 Chronicles 28:9 (author's bold)

Acknowledging God requires a mind, but David wants more than that. He wants Solomon to have a willing mind that will seek to understand God, be devoted to God and serve God. Many just acknowledge the existence of God or some gods or something of that nature. That is very different than having a willing mind to seek the one true God and love him with your whole heart/soul, mind and body. Beautiful Balance is found using our minds.

Solomon not only took his father's advice but also asked God for wisdom in 1 Kings 3. God was so impressed with such a request before Solomon would begin his rule that God granted him a wise and understanding heart, a mind to discern and make judgements and he became world renown in the arts and sciences of the day. "So, I turned my mind to understand, to investigate and to search out wisdom and the scheme of things and to understand the stupidity of wickedness and the madness of folly." Ecclesiastes 7:25

Solomon wrote the Song of Solomon, the book of Proverbs, and Ecclesiastes in the Bible. He dedicated himself to a lifetime of learning. Poetry, songs, sciences and art were just part of the gift God granted. The ability to have discernment and judgement gave King Solomon's people unprecedented peace and prosperity. It was an overflow blessing the people enjoyed from his beautiful mind. The mind is beautiful. What are you doing to keep your mind balanced and growing continually like Solomon? Is this book the first thing you have read in months? I hope not. Open your mind, it desires to grow.

David tells us that God is mindful of mankind, that God cares for us (Psalm 8:4). That is an important factor about the mind of God. God's mind brings to the surface the love and care he has for us. His care is seen in many ways by offering us eternal salvation, providing food for our bodies, challenge for our minds to think and know him, and peace for our emotions to rest in his love.

The prophet Isaiah tells us, "You will keep in perfect peace those whose **minds** are steadfast, because they trust in you." Isaiah 26:3 Isn't peace more like an emotion? Does your mind race and sometimes add anxiety to your body? Sometimes your mind never seems to shut off.

It is the powerhouse of our bodies. The mind produces those lovely little chemicals that will cause it to race and our bodies to be out of balance as well. How are you doing in the trust of God department? Complicated, we are so complicated. The mind can find peace in God, what a relief to know! It is a journey, this seeking after Beautiful Balance.

God speaks to his prophet Jeremiah and says, "I, the Lord, search the heart and examine the mind, to reward each person according to their conduct, according to what their deeds deserve." Jeremiah 17:10 Our heart/soul, mind and body are getting a close examination by God. How are you doing? Is God's love flowing through you and giving you the ability to love others and do good deeds? It all comes from the needed relationship with God.

Sometimes I think my conduct and deeds should give me a straight shot to hell. Thank God, he forgives and gets my mind, heart and body back on track to good deeds motivated by love. The verse uses the word reward, this gives it a specific direction. God is looking to 'reward', not to punish in this verse. Truly, my conduct can be very far from what it should be. I am glad that God is looking to prosper me and give me a hope and future that is eternal (Jeremiah 29:11).

The Old Testament journey puts us on a path to see the greatness of the mind. God has created each mind, heart/soul and body unique. Each person thinks, judges and perceives differently. Our upbringing and culture affect how our mind will go about making decisions, thinking and growing.

As a teacher, I know the value of a mind. Children easily desire to learn new things. They are like little sponges. Adults can take a cue from a child. One thing every teacher knows is that some children are more teachable than others. I call it the teachable spirit; coaches use a similar term and say 'coachable spirit'. Teachable kids are a teacher's joy because they are constantly using their minds. The desire to learn is gravitating them to be humble, submissive and expectant toward the teacher's authority and things they are showing the child.

As adults are we humble, submissive, and expectant toward learning from authorities in our lives? Sometimes yes, many times no. God is our most awesome authority and he has so much truth to teach us. God has given us his written word. It doesn't get any more fantastic than that! You can hear directly from God by reading his word or hearing it preached to you. Have you ever read the Bible or listened to a preacher or teacher of God's word? I recommend both, of course, as a matter of growth toward Beautiful Balance. God will speak directly to you about your personal stuff. How you need him, what areas you need growth in and you will find amazing encouragement to take on your Beautiful Balance journey. It's that good old story of Jesus, good news, salvation, forgiveness, repentance and eternal life. So, bring your mind on board this Beautiful Balance journey – think, will, perceive, imagine and judge.

New Testament Thoughts on the Mind

The New Testament has some great information about the mind. Jesus goes right to work in the gospels and challenges those who want to follow him to be doing those two greatest commandments from God – love the Lord your God with your whole heart/soul, mind and strength and love your neighbor as yourself (Matthew 22:37, Mark 12:29-31, Luke 10:27) This is where we get into the word and work of God. The mind just isn't some little think tank in our head. It is completely and thoroughly connected to our emotions and body. The mind is what produces the "do". Jesus made it clear. We are to do his command, not just think about it in our mind. Bummer, I just like thinking about what a good person I am and how much I love God, but I truly don't want to go feed that homeless guy! Busted! The mind Jesus calls us to have, will be a mind that puts self-control over our emotions and actions to our bodies. Hmmm…

Why on earth do we need self-control over our emotions? Ask any counselor, psychologist or psychiatrist. Our world is running rampant with people who have placed no self-control over themselves and it gets names and diagnosis lists like: generalized anxiety disorder, ADD, ADHD, Bipolar, defiant disorder, depression, clinical depression, personality disorder and on and on and on…You are probably carrying one of these tags. My family members certainly are, and I am not making light of it. It is so serious. Anxiety, the basis for many of the things I just listed has destroyed so many of my family members. It crushes a person with unfounded fears, smothers them with accepting less than they are and prevents them from enjoying all the good God has surrounded them with. It is the one emotion so out of control without using the mind that sends me right into 'anger mode'. It makes me angry that so many are ruined by anxiety.

Anxiety can send a person right to the addiction list for drugs, alcohol, overspending – you name it. Then the viscous cycle of dropping off begins and depression takes over when they have spent themselves out with anxiety. I don't see much difference in my unbelieving friends compared to long standing member Christians. The vicious cycle of anxiety and depression was one of the reasons I began Beautiful Balance. I saw so many lady followers of Christ walking around in a funk of anxiety and depression it made me sick. I should do something. I am. I am writing this book to get some people back on track.

The uncompromising connection is there. The mind controls the emotions. What? That is unfair, I just can't stop. Yes, Jesus says you can and he sends the rest of the writers of the New Testament to share this good news. He filled the Old Testament with good news too about commanding your emotions. David most assuredly acknowledges the emotions in his Psalms and offers control through the mind and a steadfast knowledge of God through his word.

I won't go off on some kick about discontinuing your psych meds. The situation is too complex, and I am no medical doctor. I will say here that you must go to God, go to his word and look there to begin gaining balance. Do you even know what self-control is? My phone dictionary says it is control or restraint of oneself or one's actions or emotions. Spirit-mind-body, self-control goes over all three. It's a wee little concept that is huge for Beautiful Balance.

The proverbs (Proverbs 16:32, 25:18) talk about self-control by comparing it to a person who has none. It is like a warrior that smashes up and destroys an entire city he just conquered. What good would that city be then? No spoils left to enjoy. No self-control leads to spiritual destruction, emotional destruction, mental destruction and physical destruction. You get the picture and your mind is probably listing some damage assessment like FEMA (Federal Emergency Management Agency) when they come in to deal with a natural disaster.

The Apostle Paul begins a preaching session to Felix, one of the Roman leaders over Jerusalem and Judea, at the time of his persecution. Paul goes on about righteousness, self-control and the judgment to come when Christ returns, and Felix sent him away (Acts 24:25). Felix just didn't want to hear about the message from Jesus. Yes, there is good news about forgiveness, salvation, and eternal life, but there is also some ownership of self-control over our spirits, minds and bodies. We will have to answer to God one day and we are headed to eternal life or eternal damnation. Self-control plays a huge part in the up or down ending.

The Apostle Paul goes on in 1 Corinthians 7:5 addressing prayer and how a man and wife can restrain themselves sexually for a while to devote themselves to prayer and pressing spiritual matters. But they must get back together in union as a man and wife, so they will not be tempted to lose self-control in that area and fall into the temptation of sin surrounding adultery. It is so important, this concept of self-control.

Paul sends letters to Timothy and Titus and makes it clear that anyone who will be called to or wishes to lead in God's church, must be self-controlled. We are followers of Christ and part of his church, so, much of this advice applies to everyone, not just the 'leader'. That self-control involves their spiritual life, they need to show the ability and desire to grow in the knowledge of God's word, be filled with the Holy Spirit and walk accountably with Jesus as their Lord and Savior.

Their minds must pursue self-control, gain knowledge of the scriptures, discipline themselves to teach, and control their emotions to be temperate, holy, and faithful. Their bodies must be controlled with keeping a wife, raising children, being hospitable to others, act in love and kindness toward others, and not be greedy or unrespectable. It is always there – the balance of the whole of us – Spirit-Mind-Body.

Paul writes in Galatians and spouts out a commonly memorized verse: Galatians 5:22-23 "But the fruit of the Spirit is love, joy, peace, patience, kindness, goodness, faithfulness, gentleness, self-control. Against such there is no law." Hello! Most of the list is our heart/soul emotions in relationship with God through Jesus Christ and guess what? Self-control, that little bitty thing from the mind wraps it all up and makes it functional in Jesus. We can enjoy such a wondrous list of positive emotion and virtues and even harsher emotions when they are controlled. Jesus gives us that power by being in relationship with him.

The Apostle Peter gives self-control its very own place in his list. "For this very reason, make every effort to add to your faith, goodness; and to goodness, knowledge; and to knowledge, self-control; and to self-control, perseverance; and to perseverance, godliness; and to godliness, mutual affection; and to mutual affection, love" (2 Peter 1:5-7). The Spirit is commanded to own these emotions in our relationship with Christ, control them with our mind and use them in our bodies by loving God and others. Wow! Always balanced in Christ.

We aren't crazy people out of control. We can gain control through a spiritual relationship with Christ. Think about what the world calls 'mental illness'. It is not an illness of the mind after all.

It is an illness in the heart/soul of man. The spirit and emotional seat of man out of control is what the world labels 'mental illness'. Should you dump the meds? No way. Instead, get yourself into a serious mindset to get on a path of self-control. Biblical Counseling to help you understand this spiritual heart/soul sickness called sin, psychiatric care to monitor carefully your medications, alternative methods of learning self-control for your body and mind besides filling them with meds that have very serious side effects on our bodies.

I will recommend three other good books here: *Grace for the Afflicted*, by Matthew Stanford, *Battlefield of the Mind*, by Joyce Meyers, and *Switch on Your Brain* by Dr. Caroline Leaf. You can gain victory in self-control. Yes, you should stay on your medications and possibly create a plan to reduce them if that is realistic. Just using your mind to gain understanding in its connection to spirit and body will be a big help. Use your mind to read if you are able or use your computer or TV to watch many videos by Dr. Leaf if reading is just too difficult with your anxieties and depressive states out of control. Your body goes along for the ride in this deal, and learning to cope with your mind will also renew self-control in your physical body.

A Story of Self-control

I am going to interject a story of hope here. Yes, hope, that expectant emotion we talked about already. If you are a living breathing soul reading this book, there is hope for you in Christ in this area of the mind called self-control. A lady I will call Livy was spiraling out of control in her early teen years. Livy was diagnosed with Asperger's, ADD, ADHD, and defiant disorder. The social struggles of starting junior high along with all these other issues sent Livy right to the suicide option. It seemed a better choice than struggling constantly. Livy knew Jesus as her savior. She just knew that suicide wasn't something she should even be thinking about, but her relationship with Christ was so snuffed and stuffed down that she could not think clearly. Her parents opted for Biblical counseling combined with medications to help break the cycle of raging chemicals in her brain. Back to the whole deal again. Spirit, mind, body are always connected and when one area is out of balance it can affect every other area.

The medications did work to break some of the cycle. The story continues. Livy found solace in a great counselor who could relate well to each issue she struggled with. Livy made it through high school and then headed off to college. Crash again! Too much all at once. Growing up, trying to be independent and living away from home was just too much. It was a change so severe that sent her into a huge depression. Yes, the suicide chant began again. Family to the rescue. Saved from college and home to pass out for several months in depression. What to do? Meds were increased and then a new counselor along with didactic group therapy. Was all this Christian or biblical? No.

The didactic group therapy did wonders. It gave Livy a new way of taking steps toward self-control. She could understand what triggered her anxiety and depressions. She could learn to master self-control and better use of social skill sets she practiced on family. She could see a light at the end of the tunnel.

But… the meds were making her emotionless. Robotic. Apathetic. Hmm, the world could be going to hell-in-a-handbasket and Livy really could care less. Something had to give. Months after the big college crash she began weaning down off all her medications. Family knew, counselors knew, and psychiatrist knew. Only family was ready to go for it. The professionals were all about the drugs and never gave a thought to the amazing ability a person has in self-control.

The feelings and emotions returned after months of weaning down. Therapy and listening closely to her mind and body gave her back control. Self-control. She could rage a little now and get a grip. She could love again and feel it, really feel it. She could care about the world going to hell in a handbasket and do something about it. She could start to get a little depressed, recognize it and makes steps to fight it. She could say along with King David, "I praise you because I am **fearfully and wonderfully made**; your works are wonderful, I know that full well" (Psalm 139:14).

I love Livy's story. No, not all of you will be able to be med-free but many of you can set a plan in place with God's loving guidance, family and friend support and professional support and gain some self-control. It will bring you closer to the Beautiful Balance we are longing for in Christ Jesus.

More thoughts on Self-control

God has given us a spirit of self-control. It takes me to the key verse my younger daughter experienced at Camp Venango for Jesus this year. Coolest Jesus camp ever. $20 still in 2017, isn't that amazing?

"For God has not given us a spirit of fear, but of power and of love and of a sound mind." (2 Timothy 1:7, NKJV)

"For God gave us a spirit not of fear but of power and love and self-control." (ESV)

What is fear? It is that lurking anxiety emotion that spirals into depression that spirals into the suicide whispers. It is an emotion that reaps a harvest of serious damage when left unchecked in the self-control department.

A cobra is about to bite you – the real flight or fight emotion of instant anxiety will save your life. The deadly and creeping emotion of generalized anxiety over every little detail in life you cannot control will smother you.

The verse reminds me of a truth of God. The power you have is in you. It is called the Holy Spirit and you receive it when you become a believer of Jesus Christ. You are sealed with the Holy Spirit, forever as God's child from that moment onward (Ephesians 1:13). That is serious spiritual power. It gives you the power to start on the path toward self-control. I love how the Apostle Paul places love before self-control. The love of God in you and the seal of the Holy Spirit over your life are powerful weapons against emotions that rage against self-control.

You are not powerless. You can begin to read scriptures and find truths to fight against emotions that are out of control. Memorize verses to give your mind clarity over emotions like fear, anxiety, depression and anger. You can gain balance. Jesus is the fulcrum of your life. Relationship in him sends you on a mission to be balanced. You are not on a teeter-totter on the playground that is always stuck up in the air. Jesus is right underneath you,

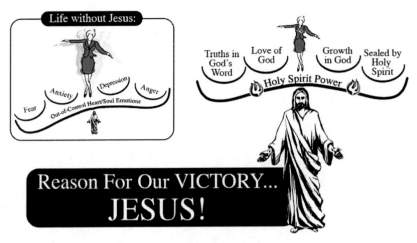

giving you the ability to get balanced.

The Holy Spirit is there too, just like the effort arm. The Holy Spirit guides and directs you to scriptures. The Holy Spirit gives you prayers to pray and prays for you when you can't even get a word out (Romans 8:26). The Holy Spirit gives you the ability to put forth the effort that leads to self-control. Amazing. God is just amazing. The balance can be gained. Thank you, Jesus, for this ability to gain self-control.

Having the Mind of Christ

Growing and gaining ground in self-control is the essential element of our mind that will bring us to understand what it means to have the mind of Christ. The Apostle Paul shares in his letter to the Corinthians:

"The person with the Spirit makes judgments about all things, but such a person is not subject to merely human judgments, for, "Who has known the mind of the Lord so as to instruct him?" But we have the mind of Christ." 1 Corinthians 2:15-16

What an amazing truth – we have the mind of Christ because the Holy Spirit is within us. This mind of Christ will guide us, give us discernment, move us toward understanding the two greatest commands, to love God wholly and love others supernaturally.

The whole chapter of Romans 8 is a great chapter of

the Bible to study about the mind of Christ and the miraculous empowerment the Holy Spirit gives to those who believe. A key verse is:

> "Those who live according to the flesh have their minds set on what the flesh desires; but those who live in accordance with the Spirit have their minds set on what the Spirit desires. The mind governed by the flesh is death, but the mind governed by the Spirit is life and peace." Romans 8:5-6

The life and peace a person experiences in having the mind of Christ is knowledge that we have eternal life, forgiveness of sins and power to become like Christ as we live out our lives in the here and now. We are spirit-minded people now, not people governed by just the flesh. Spiritual things, growth in God, and letting him transform us will quicken our heart/soul, mind and bodies. Instant satisfaction of just our bodies or minds, things of this world that will not last, won't be as inviting to us.

Beautiful Mind

Being governed by just the flesh, desiring things that are not godly, leads to death. Never turning from that fleshly mind and body will prevent a relationship from ever forming with Jesus. As a new Christian, you may find that old habits and a mind moved toward fleshly living are hard to break. But we have the mind of Christ and self-control with Holy Spirit power to fight for balance in this Jesus we love so dearly.

> "You, however, are not in the realm of the flesh but are in the realm of the Spirit, if indeed the Spirit of God lives in you. And if anyone does not have the Spirit of Christ, they do not belong to Christ. But if Christ is in you, then even though your body is subject to death because of sin, the Spirit gives life because of righteousness. And if the Spirit of him who raised Jesus from the dead is living in you, he who raised Christ

from the dead will also give life to your mortal bodies because of his Spirit who lives in you." Romans 8:9-11

The more you read God's word, listen to preaching and teaching, attend church or small group Bible study, the more of Christ's mind you will have. Victory will be won, one small battle at a time.

What else goes along with this mind of Christ? Wisdom. And with it come discernment, understanding, and knowledge. The Bible tells us the fear of the Lord is the beginning of wisdom and all his precepts have good understanding (Psalm 111:10). Your relationship with Christ is there, you feel it in your heart/soul, know it in your mind and now you can feed it and find balance in it by reading God's word and having it poured into you any way you can get it. God's word has the wisdom and promises that continually hold you in balance.

You don't always feel like it's a real relationship. Feelings and emotions are subject to our humanity and frail nature. Our heart/soul is a gift from God and our emotions are wonderful, but they can be tricky and get us off balance. So, your mind and self-control and some Holy Spirit wisdom are needed on a regular basis to keep you growing in this mind of Christ and keep the feelings reminded of the truths in God's word.

The Apostle Paul prays and asks for wisdom to be given to new believers (Colossians 1:9, Philippians 1:9-11). We can pray and ask God for wisdom as well. The Apostle James tells us:

"If any of you lacks wisdom, you should ask God, who gives generously to all without finding fault, and it will be given to you" James 1:5.

Wisdom from God, with self-control and the Holy Spirit in you giving you the mind of Christ, is a powerful combination to keep balanced. This wisdom also serves as a guide and protector to keep you using the mind of Christ and turning away from the mind set on fleshly or worldly things. God has given us all the equipment we need to stay balanced.

Wisdom is also found in good counsel from godly pastors, church leaders and fine older people in our lives, parents, siblings, a boss, a mentor at work, etc. It serves you well to seek out counsel from others you see as 'wise'. "Plans fail for lack of counsel, but with many advisers they succeed." Proverbs 15:22 Use the wisdom of God and the power of the Holy Spirit to sift through 'good advice' or wisdom offered by others. "I will instruct you and teach you in the way you should go; I will counsel you with my loving eye on you." Psalm 32:8 God cares about covering every detail you need to stay beautifully balanced.

Unity and the Mind

Your mind is growing, and you are seeing things from Christ's point of view now. You are using self-control, gaining the mind of Christ, experiencing God's wisdom. Something I found fascinating while studying the mind and scriptures is that unity is a theme throughout the Old and New Testaments when it comes to the mind. This mind of God and Christ wishes for unity with the people of God and himself. Thinking on the same things, moving toward doing things God would want.

The Old Testament story of Moses and the designing and making of the Tabernacle is a great example of seeing unity of the mind. The people were of one mind and heart and gave so many offerings to see the Tabernacle completed that they had to be restrained from bringing more. (Exodus 36:6-7) How wonderful to be part of something that is more than just yourself. I hope you have experienced that kind of unity of the mind that compels God's people to act sacrificially and generously. I have seen it time and time again in my own life. One of God's people has an 'idea', it grows, and others unify with the project or calling. and amazing results happen. The money is found, a building is located, property is donated – whatever it is, when God is moving the minds of his people to be unified, the miraculous and amazing surround it.

King David needed the unity of the mind that only God could give to unite the entire country. He had been chased and pursued by King Saul, his mentor and beloved leader. Saul was losing the kingdom to David because he did not have God's mind. David was gaining it because he had the heart of God and a desire to create unity with the mind of God.

"He won over the hearts **of** the men **of** Judah so that they

were all of **one mind**. They sent word to the king, "Return, you and all your men." 2 Samuel 19:14

"All these were fighting men who volunteered to serve in the ranks. They came to Hebron fully determined to make David king over all Israel. All the rest of the Israelites were also of one mind to make David king." 1 Chronicles 12:38

Having the mind of God is powerful. David united an entire country with it. He handed a united country over to his son Solomon and began the legacy of seeing God's Holy Temple built in Jerusalem with that unity.

The entire Christian church was built on that concept of being of one mind. "All the believers **were one** in heart and **mind**. No **one**, claimed that any **of** their possessions was their own, but they shared everything they had." Acts 4:32 The entire little band of Jesus disciples had gathered together after he had ascended to heaven and gave them instructions to wait to receive the Holy Spirit. The outpouring of the Holy Spirit on Pentecost created the unity of heart/soul, mind and body that sent the little rag-tag group to the ends of the earth preaching the good news of Jesus. That Holy Spirit they received, I received, you have received. He is active and living in you, giving you the mind of Christ and the ability to have unity with Christ and Christ's people. Amazing.

The unity of mind you have with Jesus sends you to a place where you can find your balance in him. He knows you. He wants you to know him. You can understand how to love God with your whole heart/soul, mind, and body. You are equipped to follow the second command as well, to love others supernaturally. The two commands go together, just like you are a whole heart/soul, mind and body. You can't love God and then hate your neighbor. It is just not possible. There are days that you may struggle to do the second command well, but down in the depths of your heart/soul, Jesus and this awesome Holy Spirit are working a transformation on you. It is much better than any surface beauty treatment you have ever had. A make-over of grand heavenly scale is in the works on your whole self, Spirit-Mind-Body. Unity is rich, and it is part of the story of gaining Beautiful Balance.

Renewing of Your Mind

Romans 12:2 says: "Do not conform any longer to the pattern of this world, but be transformed by the renewing of your mind. Then you will be able to test and approve God's will is his good pleasing and perfect will." God's will, is not a mystery. Jesus gave it to us in our key verse of Mark 12:20-31 "the most important one," Jesus answered, "is this: Hear O Israel, the Lord our God, The Lord is One. Love the Lord your God with all your heart and with all your soul and with all your mind and with all your strength. And the second is this: Love your neighbor as yourself. There is no commandment greater than these." You are out and about doing God's will as you learn about him, understand how to love him from studying his word and do your best each day to let that love well up and out to love others.

The Holy Spirit plays a part in renewing the mind. You must actively engage in reading and studying God's word. You are part of this relationship, not just some passive person watching the movie of your life with God pass you by. I will put a plug in here for reading other works as well. I am taking some of the information from *Spiritual Leadership* by J. Oswald Sanders (1994, Moody Press). Yep, you caught me reading again. I am an ultra-nerd and love to read. Reading is a great way to renew your mind. It stimulates you to think, reason, perceive and ponder.

The Apostle Paul was concerned that Timothy bring his parchments (2 Timothy 4:13). Paul spent the first three years after becoming a Christian, studying and preaching (Galatians 1:17-18) then spent another 14 years studying the scriptures (Galatians 2:1) after he had already spent the beginning part of his 30 some years studying to begin with! Paul's study would have included all the scriptures and all the ancient philosophers etc. No wonder God called this man to be the one to take the good news of Jesus to the gentiles. He knew his stuff because he was a serious student of reading, learning and renewing his mind.

Read the Bible. That is a priority. Study it. Know it because knowing it gives you access into this love relationship with God through Jesus Christ. The Bible tells us that: "In the beginning was the Word, and the Word was with God, and the Word was God." John 1:1 "The Word became Flesh and made his dwelling among us. We have seen his glory, the glory of the One and Only, who came from the Father, full of grace and truth." John 1:14 The Word is Jesus, God in the Flesh! Ponder that a minute – no – how about you ponder that for your lifetime.

Jesus is this Son of God, God in the flesh, who was from the beginning and has no ending. Jesus, who spoke his word in the beginning and created all life (Genesis 1-3). The Words in the Bible are his words, he is the Word. Did you ever think about the privilege you have in owning a Bible? Reading a Bible? Holding it in your hands? The Word is God and his very nature is in that Bible. The Holy Spirit reveals the love of God, the person of God and the plan of God for you in that Bible.

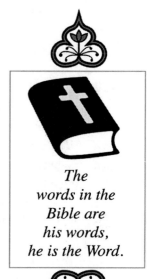

The words in the Bible are his words, he is the Word.

I love the Word of God. I swim in it, immerse myself in it. God's love and purposes for my life are wrapped in it. God blessed me with one purpose many years ago. He blessed me with the ability to read his word and write a devotional from it. That is, by the power of the Holy Spirit a work in my life. Not of my own power or choosing. I am blessed to strive in my purpose and take the challenge of writing this book, Beautiful Balance. I love to read and from my reading flows the gift of writing. It's beautiful and it's balanced in Christ.

I do read many other books. In *Spiritual Leadership* Sanders mentions that many of the great saints and missionaries of the past not only were students of the Bible but had a handful of specific works or writers that they would go to for encouragement, thought and challenge. I find that to be true of my life. Ministry speaking, I gravitate toward reading Amy Carmichael, Mother Teresa, Adoniram Judson and William Carey. Why? The country of my heart and soul is India.

My youngest daughter is adopted from India. Maybe all

the reading I did in my younger years as a baby Christian spurred me on by the Holy Spirit to give my heart to this country.

Spiritually, I am uplifted by reading Charles Spurgeon. I have his entire collection of sermons and love to read them. I love to read biographies of great preachers like George Whitefield and Jonathan Edwards. I read thought provoking works by C.S. Lewis.

Entertainment wise, I am enamored by J.R.R. Tolkien and his classics *The Lord of the Rings* and *The Hobbit*. Good fantasy and stimulating science fiction capture my imagination when I read.

There is a theme with my reading. It goes back to our verse in Romans. Do not be conformed to the pattern of this world. It also goes back to the Romans chapter 8 verses. I do not want to be fleshly and spend my time reading or doing other things of this world that have very little spiritual renewal or growth to my heart/soul, mind and body. I don't read about garbage like sexually immoral things. Toss the book out if you start reading and it seems interesting only to bait and hook you into the smut many chapters later. Don't finish reading garbage, you will only add to the fleshly struggle in your life.

Do what Paul says in Philippians 4:8-9 "Finally, brothers, whatever is true, whatever is noble, whatever is right, whatever is pure, whatever is lovely, whatever is admirable—if anything is excellent or praiseworthy—think about such things." This is a great filter verse to help keep you from falling into the pattern of the world. Fall into the pattern of God, the Beautiful Balance of knowing Jesus. Trust the Holy Spirit to lead you into good things that will grow your Christian walk. The Holy Spirit will give you power to say 'no' to the pattern of this world and all the junk that can bring you down.

Reading and everything else that is good, praiseworthy and excellent can become part of your life. Let the Holy Spirit give you self-control, the mind of Christ, wisdom, unity of the mind with Christ and the ability to renew your mind in Christ. The balance is there. It is found in relationship. Finding your purpose in God's two greatest commandments is the Beautiful Balance. Jesus is holding you up.

The Mind and Decision Making

I had to put this section in here by the mind. You make so many decisions each day you never even give a thought to how much your mind is working on your behalf. Our minds are amazing. Should I have white toast or wheat? Bacon or sausage? Eggs over easy or scrambled? That is just the pre-breakfast decision making. My first decision in the morning with my husband is what is the workout for the day video? Yes, we try and get up at 5 am each day and workout. More on that in the last part of the book on our body.

I am not going to go into all the fascinating science behind decision making and the mind and the body. The billions of neurons blasting away in your brain, sending signals and chemicals streaming through your body…You get it. Always connected this whole self of ours. Your mind begins the process for decision making but your heart/soul emotion center and body come into the processes also. The mind perceives and processes, thinks and assess. Your emotions weigh in and feel it. Your body may feel it with elation, a nervous tingling or heart palpitations! Depending on the severity of a decision at hand.

We have all been there. Breakfast decisions are not such a big deal. We go about taking the food out of the fridge that suited our fancy for the moment and pop it into our mouths without a thought of how much mind power that just took up. Cool. But what about decisions that are a bit bigger than breakfast? Like buying a house, a car, having a baby? Whoa. Stop right there. Big decision alert.

I even made the decision to go back to school a couple of years ago. I weighed in many choices, pharmacy school, masters in microbiology…hmmm…this masters in organizational leadership sounds interesting. Wow, it's what I have been doing these last 25 years as a stay at home mom, running a house, six kids, a hubby and being on many community committees. Topping it off with running my own business, I could do that. I would like to refine my skill set in that area. Decision made.

Not so easy. I did consult a wide variety of individuals—like my hubby, six kids, sister, best friends and mom. I did listen to the

Holy Spirit, who directed me to the major in the first place. I prayed, I fasted, I interviewed at the school. I was nervous in my mind and body. I had crazy emotions like bawling fits because I didn't have confidence to do something so big. And the cost? Yeah that. I stepped out in faith to do the schooling and it cost me $30,000. Yes, I am still paying for it. Was it a bad decision? Sometimes I don't know. It gave me the confidence to write more and this book is a result. How will I finance this book's publication? I don't know. I will put an excerpt in my book to let you know. No, I haven't landed a fulltime job. The degree has been a detriment in that area – I'm too over qualified now to work hard and do a good job for some company. And I guess I'm an old lady too. I will talk more about the benefits I gained from my degree in my last section on imagination. Decisions are not always fully realized right when we make them.

So, when I went to write this section of my book I asked my family members at the dinner table to suggest a Bible story to use that involved decision-making. Hand's down it was Adam and Eve and the blasted bad decision they made that sent the whole world into sin and separation from God. Why did they make such a bad decision, I pondered?

It goes back to what we have been learning about our mind. Self-control was a little low and the serpent sounded so crafty. Will I really be like God? The whole love God with their whole heart thing was a little lacking too. Is God holding back on us? No mind of God, no unity with God, no wisdom in trusting God. And no renewing the mind with God.

Maybe their minds were just too new; babies in this new created world? Nice try. They had the breath and spirit of God himself. Same as us. Each human being is created in God's image and has the capability to know Him. He planned it that way. We can also reject the creator who made us. We can grab the fruit like Adam and Eve, and pass on all it means to love God with our whole heart/soul, mind and body. We can take less and believe the serpent and the lie that we can be like God. Be like God – Yes, I am a god! That is what the world tells us. Part of that fleshy stuff and conforming to the world, that the serpent seethed out to Eve.

No, I do not have to make bad decisions. I have the Holy Spirit of God in me. Jesus sent him to earth to be poured out on everyone who calls on the name of the Lord. I am not God. I am made in his image and have superior access to the God of the Universe. Paul reminded the Corinthians in his letter:

> "However, as it is written: 'What no eye has seen, what no ear has heard, and what no human mind has conceived'—the things God has prepared for those who love him" (1 Corinthians 1:9).

Finding beautiful balance with this God of the Universe is so magnificent that the mind and body can't even comprehend it. And we think we are so smart as to call ourselves, gods!

God loves us fully in the created beings that we are. God makes no mistakes. He made each of us just the way he designed. He has given each the capacity to decide to follow or reject him. He has given each the capability to make sound decisions here on earth as his followers.

Are you reeling from a bad decision? The consequences just keep pouring in. Stop right here and make an assessment with this wonderful mind God has given you. Go back over it one more time and list the reasons why it wasn't so good. Did you know God at the time? I mean really know him and have the Holy Spirit within you for some guidance? Even goody, goody Christians make bad choices – remember King David and that little lady Bathsheba we mentioned earlier? Did you pray, seek counsel from the Holy Spirit, God, his word, others? I am assuming you will find that some key points and parts for making a better or wise decision were missing from your decision.

What do you do now? All those things you just listed that were missing from the bad decision, make a point of getting those together for the next decision. God is a giver of second, third and endless chances, if need be. But should we keep going beyond a second, third, or fourth chance? Maybe we should start putting our minds to work with the self-control we need to be better decision makers. God has equipped us. The Holy Spirit is there, wisdom is there, God is there.

I want to interject some more on wisdom here from the book of James.

> "Who is wise and understanding among you? Let them show it by their good life, by deeds done in the humility that comes from wisdom. But if you harbor bitter envy and selfish ambition in your hearts, do not boast about it or deny the truth. Such "wisdom" does not come down from heaven but is earthly, unspiritual, demonic. For where you have envy and selfish ambition, there you find disorder and every evil practice. But the wisdom that comes from heaven is first of all pure; then peaceloving, considerate, submissive, full of mercy and good fruit, impartial and sincere. Peacemakers who sow in peace reap a harvest of righteousness. James 3:13-18

James mentions the selfish ambition and envy that got Adam and Eve into trouble. Your bad decisions may be just part of that old self, that self which desires to 'be god'. Fleshly, earthly, unspiritual and downright demonic. Scripture writers don't hold back. We don't need any of that earthly wisdom that is floating about in droves. Earthly wisdom is driving the pattern of this world. It tells young people they can be whatever sex they 'choose' or 'feel like' today. It tells young ladies to end their pregnancies because it's just a 'blob of tissue' and not a precious baby, so, who needs the bother? It tells people to take 'another hit' because the anxiety is just too much to cope with.

The wisdom of God, which people can ask for, is so much different. You need it to get on a path of sound decision-making. Godly decision-making. Spirit, mind and body balanced decision making. Look at this spiritual, heart/soul list: pure, peace-loving, considerate, submissive, full of mercy, good fruit (meaning spiritual fruit, Christ-minded stuff), impartial and sincere. This wisdom from God is good stuff. And you know what else? Those who use it can lay out their lives with peace and reap righteousness from it. That is what we are looking for, some ability to make good decisions based on God's wisdom.

The wisdom we find in God's two greatest command-ments will give great benefit to our lives if we are willing to follow it. Are you ready to ask for it? God cares for you so much more in this relationship than you will ever be able to express back to him. No eye, no ear, truly our minds cannot grasp the things God has prepared for us because of his great love for us. Shocking!

One of my favorite Bible stories involves some good deci-sion making. Joshua was appointed the new leader of the Israelite people by God because he was a man of God, a sound follower with abilities to lead which Moses had groomed for many years. After the people had crossed over into their new land and had the opportunity to settle, Joshua gave them options for a decision. He reminded the people of their history with God, their great victo-ries because God did the fighting, the miracles they had witnessed, etc. Then he gave them choices. They could either follow the gods of their old ancestors prior to Abraham, the gods of Egypt where they had been slaves, or the gods of the people of the new land, or they could follow the one true God who had shown himself faithful and fulfilled every promise ever spoken to them.

Joshua boldly proclaimed his decision, "But as for me and my household, we will serve the Lord." Joshua 24:15 The choices are before us every day. What gods will we follow? Idols of our ancestors, money and pleasure (very popular gods today), fame, power and godlike status in my eyes and in others' eyes. Joshua went with that Holy Spirit conviction to go after the one true God. Joshua made a right decision. We can too. The wisdom from God is there. The Holy Spirit power and conviction are there. The mind of Christ and his unity, all of it is there for us. Beautiful Balance.

The Mind and our Imagination

Whew! Our minds are busy learning self-control, wisdom, unity, having the mind of Christ, discovering God's love in his Word, and making decisions to name a few of our cool mind culti-vating beautiful balance truths. What about the other few minutes of free time our minds might have in a day? Do you ever wonder? One of my favorite questions is that you can fill in the blank with anything that you have ever wondered. How many stars are in the sky? How many hairs are on your head? Did you ever wonder that if you could fly how everything would look like from on high?

The Apostle Peter quoted a wonderment verse from the book of Joel for the people in Jerusalem shortly after the Holy Spirit fire filling from Pentecost.

> "In the last days, God says, I will pour out my Spirit on all people. **Your** sons and daughters **will** prophesy, **your young men** will see visions; **your** old **men will dream dreams**. Even on my servants, both men and women, I will pour out my Spirit in those days, and they will prophesy. I will show wonders in the heavens above and signs on the earth below, blood and fire and billows of smoke. The sun will be turned to darkness and the moon to blood before the coming of the great and glorious day of the Lord. And everyone who calls on the name of the Lord will be saved." Acts 2:17-21, Joel 2:28-32 (author's bold)

About three thousand people came to know Jesus as their savior that day after Peter preached. That is the amazing power of the Holy Spirit in a person who is yielded to be used.

Dreams, visions, imagination. Stuff you don't hear preached about often, or maybe never in your church. I am a child at heart. Maybe that is why I can love Jesus so easily. I have a vivid imagination and always have. I do believe God's gift of the ability to read and love of reading fostered my imagination to this day. Reading took me to the far reaches of outer space, to the cool and dark places in the jungles of India, to the plains of north America riding the wind on my painted pony…

My imagination gave me belief in this awesome Jesus who could work miracles like no other. What a cool God! I believed what I read in the Bible as a child and what my Sunday school teachers took the time to teach. I especially loved this one children's Bible my parents had at home with great pictures and art work depicting the amazing stories from the Bible. See it in your mind's eye-imagination. We are so gifted by God to have this amazing ability.

Imagination is the deep stuff of the heart and soul. It fuels creativity for artists, musicians and poets and writers like me. It gives people gifted in finance to make zillions of dollars and architects to build skyscrapers. It takes children on vast and wondrous trips while reading a book. I was a cop, a robber, a spaceman, Wonder Woman, Aqua man, a veterinarian, and the next gold medal gymnast! My childhood was filled with the stuff of imagination. I even had an imaginary friend.

I have early memories of sitting on my daddy's lap reading books to him. Yes, I think I could read very young. And yes, I had a daddy, not a dad, just to clarify. I remember him telling me, "You can be anything you want, we live in America." I didn't get the gist of that until I was older and understood it came from a man who was a first-generation Slovak immigrant, so proud to be in America. Thanks, Daddy, I still believe that I can be anything God wants me to be. Not just what I want, but what he wants for the purposes of my life.

Do you ever wonder? How is your imagination? Do you believe that God has unbelievable things for you and a specific purpose designed just for you? Do you ever dream dreams and have visions? I do. Wow, I could share some doozies with you. The space of my mind is vivid and ripe with ideas, dreams, visions and inspirations. These words flow out of that space in my brain. I have been writing my ideas, dreams and visions down for years. It inspires me and moves me to the next good work God has for me (Ephesians 2:10).

My favorite story to share about a dream is this: It was late one night about 2 AM and I was awakened by the clear crying of my baby. It was coming from our little girl's empty crib in the connecting room where our older daughter was sound asleep. You see, that empty crib was the crib waiting for our baby girl from India. The Holy Spirit spoke so clearly to me and said, "Get up and pray. Your baby girl is hurt and needs you to pray." I jumped out of bed like any fierce and protective mother. I spent the next four hours in prayer on my knees pleading in intercession for the baby girl I hadn't even been matched up with. That's right, we were just into the adoption process of a long wait and hadn't even matched with our little girl. She was nameless and faceless. but her cries in the night were just as if she were right in that crib. Our minds are amazing and the prompting of the Holy Spirit through the imagination engine of our brains works with God to accomplish his good purposes in our lives and in his kingdom work.

Months later when we matched with our girl, her paper work revealed a stunning bit of information. The very night I spent obeying the voice of the Holy Spirit somehow the femur of her right leg was broken in the orphanage at about three months of age. What a glorious confirmation that this little sweetie was my baby! She had been hurt and she did need her mother's intercessory prayers. None other would do and I was glad to oblige the Spirit of God.

How on earth do we tap into this amazing place called imagination? You must begin by fueling the imagination. Most adults are just dull. They lose that ability to dream and imagine as the responsibilities of life take over. I can still be silly and create crazy scenarios in my mind.

My kids grew up playing and using vivid imaginations because I encouraged it. Let's build a fort in the living room and have a battle like king Arthur's knights! Let's take these Bocce balls and pretend they are dinosaur eggs and we are dinosaurs protecting the last of our race. Let's use the bunk bed to be our pirate ship and sail the seven seas! Cool stuff huh! I can't wait to have grandkids, I will do it all over again!

Go back to those crazy kid days. Fuel your imagination. Set up a crazy question as if you had all the money in the world …or if you had three wishes what would they be? You can do it. Here it comes – read the Bible! Let those amazing stories from the Old Testament and Miracles Jesus did in the New Testament fuel your imagination in God. We serve a God who can do the impossible. Yeah, like Jesus was born of a virgin for instance. That is God himself came down, the Word became flesh. If that doesn't get you going I am not sure what else might help.

Fuel your imagination with the godly, righteous, pure excellent thoughts of awesome things like in Philippians 4:8-9.

Do you know what else that does? Imagination grows your faith. Imagination borders on belief and faith. I imagined I could go back to college. I saw myself doing it. It fueled my faith to attempt something I saw as very difficult or maybe even impossible of myself but with God, maybe I could!

Who are some great Bible characters which experienced dreams and visions to the max? Abraham, saw God and some teams of angels a few times. He did what God asked in his vision about sacrificing his son and ended being the great-great-great far off relative of God himself when he came down as Jesus.

Joseph is one. Saved his entire people group because he let God interpret Pharaoh's dream. That is amazing imagination stuff. How about David? God spoke to him in dreams and visions and gave David the gift of poetry and prophecy and he wrote about Jesus coming all those far off years before.

And Daniel, my most beloved dreamer and visionary. He was God's most beloved as well and God told him that, "O man most highly esteemed" Daniel 9:23, 10:19 when he sent angels to share visions with Daniel. Daniel, a boy who was plucked from Israel and taken captive to Babylon lived to be one of God's most beloved recipients of dreams and visions. Daniel lived to see several kingdoms rise and fall in his lifetime. Babylon, the Medes and Persians. He served in major leadership positions, second to the emperor even, because he was receptive in his mind for what God would reveal to him. He was a willing servant to be balanced in the creator of the Universe.

Jesus' own earthly father, Joseph, responded to the dream God gave him for protection. Leave the land and go to Egypt to keep the boy safe (Matthew 2). He married Mary, the virgin mother of Jesus, on the prompting of dreams and Holy Spirit guidance (Matthew 1).

Many stories in the New Testament involve dreams and visions with Jesus, his disciples and newly appointed apostles. Each responded with wisdom and prompting from the Holy Spirit. And what is a common theme, is that every dream and vision is godly and good? All the information and promptings in those dreams and visions were about God doing his work on earth through human vessels. Each was only asked to do something that lined up in accordance with God's word.

Open your mind to the endless possibilities of an imagination gifted to you by God.

You can't say a dream or vision is of God if it directs you to do something ungodly. I will share an example. I met a man once who felt called to be a missionary to India. He was sure. It was in a dream. He set out to do all he could to get there including divorcing his wife of 30 years who for some reason didn't get the 'dream' notice from God. No support from me. It was not a dream of my God. You don't divorce your wife and take off to India because the God of the Bible doesn't direct anything contrary to proper Bible information. A man is to be married to one wife, for life. Jesus even preached on it in Matthew 19.

Be willing to imagine. Be willing to examine dreams and visions. They must align with God's word. God's kingdom is to thrive for them, you are to be built up as a believer for them and others are not to be harmed in any way from them.

Open your mind to the endless possibilities of an imagination gifted to you by God. Let your Beautiful Balance be full and powerful, moving to the depths of your mind by the God of the Universe who created and designed you to imagine. I am excited for you. I can't wait to hear from you about where God's purposes led you to go through using your imagination and all the creativity it opened!

Think about all the inventions we have seen in the last 200 years. Even the development of the huge corporations and vast millions of dollars floating in the world today started from someone's dream. Those folks let their imaginations take them to a place that God used for the good of many. You see, God's goodness is throughout all the earth. Sometimes you just aren't seeing how he is playing that out. Get ready to go in the phrase of Star Trek and go where "no man has gone before." Should I make it the politically correct statement they changed it to "go where no one has gone before." Ladies or gents, get your imaginations primed and moving in the power of an awesome God.

CHAPTER SIX

◄◄✐➤ The Body ◄◄➤➤

Now we move on to the last in Jesus' statement on loving God. Love God with our whole strength. The body. I think Jesus put it last in the list because it is not the most necessary. It is important because he stressed it, but getting the heart/soul, and mind in balance under him is going to give us the most balance. It will give some relief here to those whose bodies are not whole in any way because of disease, accident or other.

Women most of all do not like this subject – the body. We stress over our bodies. Men have increased in their body stress these last 20 years, too. We don't like to talk about our bodies because it goes back to the big mind issue I wrote about first, self-control! We must take self control, responsibility, and make wise decisions about our bodies! People just don't like that.

A key verse I will impress from the scriptures is:

"Do you not know that your bodies are temples of the Holy Spirit, who is in you, whom you have received from God? You are not your own; you were bought at a price. Therefore, honor God with your bodies." 1 Corinthians 6:19-20

The Holy Spirit of God, who gives us the balance to walk in the commands of Jesus is housed in your physical body. And it's not housed in your body like a house where you are going to kick back on the couch, eat a mountain of popcorn and watch a mindless movie! The Holy Spirit is housed in a body that is like a temple.

What on earth is a temple? Even if you are not from a culture where you see temples, you have spectacular churches and cathedrals to look upon. If you have never been in a church, temple, or cathedral, take a YouTube tour of one online! The internet has cool video productions of the Temple from Jesus' day and the Apostle's day to which they refer when they talk about "temple". We just finished imagination and I need you to get God's Temple or what historians refer to as Solomon's Temple, in 'your mind's eye'! Read the details about the Temple in the Bible in 1 Kings. Do some visual if reading is a stretch for you and watch those videos!

King David, the man after God's own heart wanted to build God a temple (2 Samuel 7) but instead God allotted the task to David's son who succeeded him, King Solomon. David made provisions and donations of much of his wealth to go into the project of building the temple. Solomon was faithful and gifted by God to carry out an 'inspiration or the wondrous imagination' of David. You see how God is always at work in heart/soul, mind and body. God's plans and goodness sometimes stretch into another generation.

God's temple was spectacular! Of course, would David and Solomon have wanted otherwise? Grand, covered in gold and all the finest woods and craftsmanship went into it. It was beautiful to behold and Kings and Rulers from other nations wanted to come and see it. God however, did remind David in 2 Samuel 7, that he did not need a physical place to reside.

Jesus came and confounded the religious leaders of his day and told them he would destroy God's temple and rebuild it in three days (John 2:19). What was he talking about? Jesus did destroy God's temple in a sense. Jesus was God in the flesh and he let himself be sacrificed unto death on the cross. He was placed in a tomb, dead. Three days later he arose from the grave! Now that's good news. Now God's temple was no longer the physical location of Solomon's temple. Jesus got up from that grave and the temple (his own self) went out and about doing kingdom work, showing himself to many disciples before he ascended back to heaven.

And what did Jesus leave us? The Holy Spirit, that part of the awesomeness or Temple of God so to speak. The mysterious and almost impossible to explain work of the Holy Spirit taking up residence in anyone who calls upon the name of Jesus. The kingdom work of God is still going on today because each person who believes in Jesus receives from him their portion of the Holy Spirit, his Spirit into their own bodies.

Jesus told the woman at the well that one day God's true worshippers would worship him in Spirit and truth (John 4). That day is today. All who have the Holy Spirit of God residing in their bodies can worship in Spirit and Truth. So, you are not your own. You were bought with that price of Jesus sacrifice and resurrection and offer of salvation from it.

Your body is the Temple of the Holy Spirit. I hope this visual is sinking in now. I named this book and ministry Beautiful Balance for a reason. God's physical temple on the earth in Jerusalem was a beautiful place. You are God's mobile temple, Holy Spirit Houser, beautiful beyond compare, placed exactly where God wants to serve the purposes of his kingdom work through your life. You represent Jesus, the Christ. You, your body represents the Son of God, God in the flesh, come down to men. Is it getting in there, into that mind housed in your body.

Your Body

This is a depiction of Solomon's temple and the grandeur of it. This is what should be coming into our mind – gold, beauty, perfect architecture.

Your physical body houses the Holy Spirit of the God of the Universe! That is amazing, miraculous and a bit overwhelming.

Do you see now, why we must talk about this last section of Jesus' command? Love God with your whole strength, your whole body, all of it. This should put a different perspective on how we are treating our bodies.

How are you doing with your body? Do you love your body and nurture it daily, thinking in your mind how the Holy Spirit lives in it? Hmm…that wholeness connection again, heart/soul, mind. When was the last time you looked in the mirror and said, "Hello, Holy Spirit, what is the business of God for the day?"

I am guessing instead you looked into the mirror and rang out a long list of criticisms about your body. Maybe your looks, those few wrinkles creeping in around your eyes, those lips that are just too large for your liking or that darn nose with that little bump you always wanted to get rid of.

And who on earth can stand to go clothes shopping and look into the huge dressing room mirror that shows us in underwear, sweating each time we have to look and see how bad the next outfit is looking? I know, I just had the laughs of my life trying on dresses for my son's wedding.

Got to get a laugh out of the back-fat creeping up out of some of those sweet dresses! Ugh! My daughter and I did laugh too! We put into godly perspective some of what I am going to discuss in this section.

This photo is not what we should be looking like as God's house. No dilapidated, run down and useless houses in God's kingdom! If your feelings are going to this place, let's get some Holy Spirit revelation back towards that temple of gold from Solomon's day!

This body of ours is a palace of gold. Are you seeing it that way? We have to use our minds here to give us a boost in the body area. You are a daughter of the King of Kings, giver of this Holy Spirit that resides in you. Daughter of the King, how have you been caring for this Holy Spirit house?

Or maybe this picture that the Apostle Paul describes

earlier in Corinthians fits in your mind better:

"But we have this treasure in jars of clay to show that this all-surpassing power is from God and not from us. We are hard pressed on every side, but not crushed; perplexed, but not in despair; persecuted, but not abandoned; struck down, but not destroyed." 2 Corinthians 4:7-9

The treasure of the Holy Spirit resides in you. You may feel like your body is not too important. Like it is a boring, unadorned jar of clay. But feelings can betray us and distract us from who we really are in Christ. If internally your jar, your body is holding the Holy Spirit you have a treasure worth sharing.

Look at the jar as if it is holding the most precious commodity in the desert. What would that be?

WATER! Are you feeling thirsty as I write this paragraph? Get out in the kitchen and run the spigot and get yourself a cool, tall glass of water. Drink deeply and think on this picture Paul is trying to paint.

Even Jesus told the Woman at the Well (John 4) she could drink and never thirst again. She could attain living water. "but whoever drinks of the water that I shall give him will never thirst. But the water that I shall give him will become in him a fountain of water springing up into everlasting life." John 4:14 (NKJV) He tells the crowds again about the living water: "Whoever believes in me, as Scripture has said, rivers of living water will flow from within them." John 7:38 Living water is our eternal life, made known to us by the power of the Holy Spirit. You will physically thirst again and go to your sink. But spiritually, you have all you need to stay refreshed, refueled and ready. You can share the precious living water you carry in the mundane jar of your body. The Holy Spirit is endlessly with you, eternally giving your heart/soul, mind and body all it needs. Others need to drink this precious treasure. Don't you want to share?

I don't need to go into each area of body health in detail. You can read books and watch videos on everything from how to brush your teeth properly to how to do your own pedicure in ten minutes. Head to toe. We have one beautiful body to take care of. Remember our heart/soul, the emotion center of our lives is housed in this beautiful body. Our brain, the actual place of our minds is here as well. Lots of reasons to take care of this bundle of muscle, bones, tissues and organs.

So, what do the experts, doctors and health gurus say about taking care of our bodies? Sleep eight hours each night, eat proper meals and drink plenty of water. See your doctor regularly and make sure you are getting proper check-ups to make sure your health is going along fine.

I like Proverbs 3:5-8:

> "Trust in the Lord with all your heart and lean not on your own understanding; in all your ways submit to him, and he will make your paths straight. Do not be wise in your own eyes; fear the Lord and shun evil. **This will bring health to your body and nourishment to your bones.**" (author's bold print)

The whole Spirit, Mind, body is enveloped in this set of verses. Our heart and soul must be in relationship with God, our minds keep us on God's path and our bodies benefit. Have you ever thought about God being a real nourishment to your bones? Doing things God's way and realizing the Holy Spirit is housed within our physical bodies does keep us going and can result in real physical nourishment and health overall.

Sleep/Rest

In sleep – how are you doing? If you are a young mom, or you are caring for a loved one who needs you, the sleep department might be a little lacking. These are natural stages of our lives that might cause a slight imbalance for a time. It is important for your body to get the physical rest it needs. You can be sleep deprived for a time but rest must come. Physical rest gives our bodies time to recharge. We grow those new cells we need and rejuvenate that mind from all the work we have been up to when we rest properly.

Is there some way you can get help if you are in a crazy stage of caregiving? Respite from a professional agency if there is a serious handicap your loved one has, or babysitting from family, friends, church members or neighbors if you have little ones. Don't let this slip. Pray to God and ask him to reveal someone or someway you can get help so you can rest.

Without rest you will start to slip up in your mind, you won't think clearly, you will start to feel physically ill and might even get very sick from letting your rest slip away. You could even endanger the very ones you are caring for because you are so tired.

Once, when returning from India, I had several layovers and then to top it off, an ice storm in Washington DC. I was going on about 36 hours of sleep loss. A lovely night spent at the airport because all flights were grounded put me at about 48 hours sleep loss by the time I arrived in Cleveland to the loving arms of my husband. I was a loony, and barely able to stand and walk to the car. I slept the whole two-hour ride home and then passed out for two days at home. I felt physically ill and could not think at all. Sleep loss is no one's friend.

"I lie down and sleep; I wake again, because the Lord sustains me." Psalm 3:5

"In peace, I will lie down and sleep, for you alone, Lord, make me dwell in safety." Psalm 4:8

God has ordained sleep for us to be sustained. When we sleep we can have peace because God is watching over us, we are safe in his care. The little child's prayer: Now I lay me down to sleep I pray the Lord my soul to keep if I should die before I wake I pray the Lord my soul to take (Early puritan version by Joseph Addison, 1711). The child's prayer is simple, and it reflects the simplest belief that if our relationship with God is secure, we can rest in peace because we will see God's face in eternity if we don't awaken on this earth.

Does fear of death haunt your sleep? Find scriptures like the Psalms above to memorize and give you peace. Do not let unfounded fears and general anxiety steal your rest.

I know that anxiety can steal your sleep. Give those out of control emotions to God in prayer. Find scriptures about which you are anxious and pray them about your situation. God hears our prayers. Praying will help you build trust in this God you cannot see but makes himself known to your heart/soul through his Holy Spirit. The comfort will come. The sleep will come.

How about rest? Is that different from sleep?

Yes, the rest talked about in the Bible is very different from physical sleep. When God was creating the Universe, he rested after each portion. Of course, God doesn't sleep because he is not human, but Spirit in nature and doesn't need physical sleep. God rested and set aside the last day of creation as a Sabbath rest.

> "It is a sign between Me and the children of Israel forever; for in six days the Lord made the heavens and the earth, and on the seventh day He rested and was refreshed.'" Exodus 31:17

Rest refreshed God. We need to be refreshed as well. The Sabbath is the holy day of worship that a believer in God must set aside to give attention to God. Some rest on Saturday night, some on Sunday morning or Sunday night. The day and time is not the issue; it's the focus on God, Jesus Christ, the Holy Spirit and our relationship with him that is important. The Old Testament understanding of Sabbath rest was that very little physical work was to be done on the chosen day. So, there is an element of physical rest to the day and spiritual focus on God to the day.

Back to the whole spirit, mind, body again. We rest, and it refreshes our heart/soul, mind and body. It is our time to love on God and be loved on in return. If you have never entered the rest of worshiping with a group of believers, do it this week. Your heart/soul, mind and body will begin to see this amazing relationship that exists between God and his people. Seek out a place that teaches the Bible and go and see what rest and worship look like.

God put his Spirit to rest on Jesus:

> "There shall come forth a Rod from the stem of Jesse, and a Branch shall grow out of his roots.
>
> The Spirit of the Lord shall rest upon Him, The Spirit of wisdom and understanding, The Spirit of counsel and might,

The Spirit of knowledge and of the fear of the Lord."
Isaiah 11:1-3

Jesus passes on to each one who follows him and believes that same Holy Spirit. We can rest and worship and with it comes wisdom, understanding, discernment, power, knowledge and relationship with him. All we need to rest and be refreshed is given.

Jesus passes on his wisdom about rest:

"Come to Me, all you who labor and are heavy laden, and I will give you rest. Take My yoke upon you and 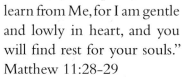 learn from Me, for I am gentle and lowly in heart, and you will find rest for your souls." Matthew 11:28-29

Rest in Christ is the heart/soul, mind and body knowing that you are his child and will be with him for eternity. It is spiritual in nature; this rest from God. Your spirit knows it. Your mind knows it. Your body knows it. It flows over and in you and gives you a spiritual refreshing that I just cannot begin to describe with words. Jesus' rest is supernatural, and it is for everyone who calls on his name.

Peter called out to the crowd at the first preaching of Jesus and said, "Repent therefore and be converted, that your sins may be blotted out, so that times of refreshing may come from the presence of the Lord," Acts 3:19 The rest and refreshment of our souls comes from the solid relationship Christ has established with us. Jesus is the Beautiful Balance. Rest and refreshing will come from him alone.

Peter gives great imagery later in his first book and says, "Therefore gird up the loins of your mind, be sober, and **rest your hope** fully upon the grace that is to be brought to you at the revelation of Jesus Christ;" I Peter 1:13 (author's bold) What a great picture of picking up our minds and literally resting them on our solid hope which is our relationship with Christ. It is something you can attain. The rest of God should be part of your relationship with him through Jesus Christ.

There is another rest I will mention as well. A physical

rest that is not sleep. I see the lack of it in the generation behind me and their children. Shall I say, "run, run, run". Who can be the busiest and have their kids in the most activities and run constantly from here to there with no rest? It is like a Star Trek episode with everyone in a time warp of running from work, to play activities, to sports activities and they are caught in non-stop motion. Childless couples and singles do the same thing.

I will grant that there will be busy seasons in a person's life. I am not knocking the wellrounded and balanced things we can do today as a family to stay healthy and grow in our spirits, minds and bodies. It can however, become out of balance very quickly, and the body pays the price but the mind and spirit suffer greatly.

Keeping a body so busy can result in creating anxiety conditions in a person's mind. ADD/ADHD can be created in a person from a lack of just sitting and resting physically. Hypermode kicks in and you find that your mind is never at rest and the vicious cycle of a busy body makes a busy mind. It is our entertainment age. Adults and kids think they must be constantly entertained. Entertainment is equated with non-stop busyness in our culture.

Christian parents don't sit with a smug smile on your face. You can be just as guilty using your list of church activities to overload your families. Don't think that just because everything you are doing is "spiritual in nature" is therefore blessing God and family. Too much kids' club, church plays, worship services 4 times a week, small groups, play groups and you name it in the name of Jesus can wipe out any family.

Common sense again. Look at your calendar. How many times a week are you running to an activity after work. Remember, you just put in an eight or ten-hour day. Maybe a bit of rest might be a good idea. Don't spiritualize on me here either and give me this line that you are listening to the Bible on audio in your car while you are running off to the next activity. I must tell you that you aren't truly focusing on the words being spoken to you, but are already engaging your mind toward the activity to come.

I recommend a couple of good books here, *First Things First*, by Stephen Covey (1994) and *Boundaries* by Dr. Henry Cloud (2009). Dr. Cloud has many books on boundaries you can choose from. Both these authors are talking about putting balance into your life through time management and gaining strength in the tiny word that can save your life: NO! Your time must be balanced. Your ability to say "no" to a long list of inviting activities can save your life.

So, how often are you running to an activity? Most of you won't believe how often you are flying like a crazed person who has caught themselves on fire and is looking for lake to jump in and get things under control. If you are running every night of the week, sometimes to more than one activity per night, you might need to assess your priorities.

Your body is not resting. You have not sat down all day to just catch your breath and rest your feet and legs. You have jammed your dinner, if you even ate, into your mouth and ran out the door from work or home if you had a second to stop. You threw the kids in the car, jamming food into their mouths on the way and screamed, "Get moving or we are going to be late!" You are teaching the cycle of, 'entertainment equals awesomeness', to the next generation with style and pizzazz.

You are wondering why your kids are freaking out on a rainy Saturday afternoon when the scheduled activity got cancelled. They come whining to you to do something. They cannot sit still. They cannot rest. And neither can you. You don't know what to do. You can't stand the sitting and you pack everyone up and go bowling.

I sympathize with the busyness. I have been there. With six kids, a mix of boys and girls, a lot of busyness has come my way. From the beginning though, rest was easy. It came through couch time reading. There are not too many other ways you can satisfy the physical touch need of a hoard of little ones. Tiny ones on your lap, toddles squeezed in close and older ones wrapped in your arms. Reading time became resting time. Our physical bodies relished the rest and our minds renewed from the tweak of imagination in the story line.

Don't be fooled that rest apart from sleep can include the 'emptying of your mind'. Our minds are always at work and need to be at a level of rest when our physical bodies are resting. Resting in God, even at the physical level, will have an element of slowing down of the mind but never an emptying. Brother Lawrence, a sixteenth century monk, recorded some of this in the little book-let, *Practicing the Presence of God* (1699 printed 2003) He learned to fill his mind with God always. During work and physical rest, he filled his thoughts of God. He found it a most practical way to live out the purposes of God in his life through the two greatest commandments.

My young children learned rest through quiet play. Imagination games, board games, and time alone for reading or sitting quietly in the yard helped. Nature was a real place for them all to renew, get physical rest from the woods around them by sitting, listening and watching for animals to appear.

The older they got the harder it was to prioritize rest. I did it though. I wanted to go with the crazed crowd of parents running, running, running but I battled against it. I started to say no more often. Our family had a rule, one sport, one season at a time. The close in age got on the same teams! Dinners were a place to rest, right after school before practices (a bonus available to stay at home moms, those with nannies or Grammys!). Bedtime prayers were rest as we sat quietly together and prayed about friends and family with their struggles and needs. Vacations and times off from sports and activities were relished as rest with reading a good book and having quiet nights at home. Ahh the need for rest!

What a travesty this refusal to take a physical rest! It is becoming an inability. A real condition that has created ADD and ADHD-like behaviors in us and our children. Rest is so simple we just won't do it. It requires our physical body to sit still a minute or so. We need much more than just a minute. We need more like 15 or 30 or 60 minutes of being still. From all the sports activities and overabundance of things that should have burned out our physical bodies, our bodies should crave some physical rest.

The craving and need for the physical rest has been blotted out by the mind. We ignored self-control and the signals from our physical bodies to take the rest when we needed it and now we put ourselves into hyper drive. We kid ourselves and say things like 'push through', 'I am the energizer bunny', or even quote a Bible verse out of context to fit our excuses and say, 'I can do all things through Christ who strengthens me'.

A body in hyper-drive will eventually break down. Aches, pains and injuries will begin to assail our bodies. Our brains will literally feel like they want to explode from the lack of rest and the hyperdrive of the mind that is now going on. Sleep will evade us, and we will get sicker and sicker.

Only you can stop the madness of a lack of rest. You looked at the overbooked calendar and you must prioritize. You must use your mind and spirit to regain balance. Prayer, seeking wisdom, working out self-control with that little word, "no" will be your allies in this battle. You must ask yourself what is truly necessary vs what is just a filler of busyness. I think you will discover that you have many more "fillers of busyness" than you thought at first.

Learn to rest. I think it is funny that I am even writing about it. Teach yourself to physically rest. Here is an easy one: lay on the floor with your butt as close to the wall as you can and stick your legs up straight against the wall. This position helps release tension in your lower back and laying will be a way to force you into a physical rest. Try this for five minutes before you fly off to the next event.

Another: go sit outside, weather permitting, close your eyes and listen intently for every sound in your neighborhood. Sit still for five minutes. I know it's killing you, but you can do it. Force yourself to engage physically in the rest. Keep going on with your rest. Practice it. You need it.

As you settle in, prioritize, say no, and begin physical rest practice you will notice that your mind will follow the pattern of rest you start to give your body. Parents you must teach your kids. They must learn to be quiet occasionally, entertain themselves with a restful activity like reading or sitting and listening to sounds outside.

Children must learn that they do not need to be on hyper drive every minute of the day and it will begin with you. They must learn to do quiet rest without you. They don't need you sitting with them every second of the day. They need to learn to have confidence in sitting in the quiet without you. Their expectation has been to have you run, run, run them everywhere, anytime non-stop. They can learn to be quiet and physically rest. You have run them so often they think they cannot sit still without you as well.

Children can learn to watch you practice rest. What makes you feel rested and calm? Do you wake before everyone else and sit quietly and sip your coffee or tea? Try doing that later in the day so your kids see you do it. Do it with them and sit and have a tea party.

Rest through worshiping God refreshes us. Rest through physically sitting or lying still refreshes us. Balance both kinds of rest in your life and your families lives. You will be refreshed, rejuvenated and renewed. Beautiful Balance in rest, it can be achieved.

Eating and Drinking and the Body

I will focus on the eating and drinking elements spelled out in the New Testament. Primarily this is because most of us reading this book won't be following any specific Old Testament Jewish food and eating guidelines. The great release from the specific Judaism food and eating guidelines was given to the Apostle Peter in the book of Acts chapter ten. Peter receives a vision from God to go and visit Cornelius, a Gentile convert to Judaism. The strict Jewish guidelines would have prevented Peter from entering the house of a non-Jew and he would not have been able to eat with him. God also gave a vision to Cornelius to send for Peter.

The Holy Spirit revealed to Peter to eat whatever he would call clean. Peter saw all kinds of forbidden or unclean Jewish animals in his vision. The vision looked like a large white sheet that was open and held all kinds of unclean animals. Peter was appalled that the Lord told him to "kill and eat" those unclean animals. The voice of the Lord said clearly, "Do not call anything impure that God has made clean." Acts 10:15

The amazing part of the story is the second blast of the Holy Spirit. Peter obeyed and went to see Cornelius. Every non-Jew who worshipped God in Cornelius's house received the powerful revelation of the Holy Spirit with fire and wind just like the apostles on Pentecost. Peter realized the vision wasn't just about food, it was about the revelation of Jesus Christ being poured out on to all who would call on God and worship him in Spirit and Truth (John 4:23), Gentiles as well as Jews.

This is good news because when it came to food and drink the non-Jews weren't following any special guidelines. In fact, they would have been taking many of the foods they had been sacrificing to idols of clay and metal and eating them up. Meat eaters, vegetarians, vegans, what have you, the food habits of all kinds would have been added to the new believers in Jesus. It is still the same today. We are only called on by one guideline in the Bible to eat in any specific manner.

The only guideline spelled out to the new gentile believers was in Acts 15. The council at Jerusalem suggested that they avoid eating foods sacrificed to idols of the other local religions, meat of strangled animals and blood from the animals. It wasn't much, but it gave some release to the Jewish followers of Jesus who would now have to embrace a new wave of people into their numbers. Sometimes compromise is a good thing. The Jews realized they had struggled with the difficulties of keeping their own rigorous laws and trying to make new converts to do the same was ridiculous.

What does some of this look like today? Pretty much you can eat and drink whatever is a part of your culture. The guideline of sacrifice to another god or idol still holds today. If you know the food you are being offered at someone's home has first been offered up to another god as a sacrifice you must clear your conscience in this matter. The Apostle Paul spent some time discussing this in 1 Corinthians 8-11. **If you are not bothered by it** and can offer up a thanks to Jesus for the sustenance set before you in that home, eat and be filled with grace and love toward your host. "So, whether you eat or drink or whatever you do, do it all for the glory of God." 1 Corinthians 10:31. If you won't offend others who are in this situation with you, eat.

But if you are bothered by it, do not eat. **Ask, before accepting** a dinner invitation and if what they serve will be offered to an idol first. Be polite and be respectful. We live in a global world, you may have many friends and neighbors who worship other gods and sacrifice their food and drink to idols first. "Everything is permissible – but not everything is beneficial" 1 Corinthians 10:23. You pass on eating or drinking that sacrificed food as a witness to those who do not know Jesus, not because you must live by a written law or code of conduct. Your kind refusal to accept the sacrificed food may help open other eyes to your love and faith in Jesus. You pass on accepting the food if others in your presence will be offended to see you eat it. Their balance in Christ might not be as secure as yours. Refuse, in order to help them grow.

That biblical stuff out of the way – let's get onto the real life in America today! All things in moderation. Or should I claim, "All things Beautifully Balanced!" That is a good saying for much of this section on the body. The Apostle Paul reminds us that all things are lawful, but not all things are helpful (1 Corinthians 6:19). It's just like all things being permissible, but not all things are beneficial. Yes, you can drink pop, or soda (if you are down south!) but how much? 3 liters a day? Or one glass? The drink is permissible, but how beneficial is it to your body's health? I think I could get on Google and find many articles to support that drinking 3 liters of pop a day is probably not beneficial to your body!

Hmmm… this means you must go back to the mind and spend some time on self-control. Are you struggling with your weight or diabetes or any number of other health issues that might find the source of discomfort in what you are eating or drinking? You know what is healthy for you by operating in self-control and common sense. No one must be a rocket scientist to get healthy. I am talking about being healthy because your body is the house of the Holy Spirit. You better be listening to God's spirit when he is speaking to you about what, how much and how often you are putting something into your body! And what about those in your life that love you? Are they trying to speak truth to you about your body care? God may be having them speak a little louder than the Holy Spirit if you have closed your mind and ears to him!

Don't ignore God. Please take a step to get balance back in your body if things are out of control! You don't need to be obsessed about the numbers on a scale, but you do need to be mindful of them if they are shouting out to you! Your body type, basic structure of large boned, medium, or petite will give some meaning to the numbers on the scale. A lady who is five feet ten inches tall and large boned can hit a nice 200 pounds and be healthy. A lady who is four feet ten and petite in body should not weigh 200 pounds. Common sense rules here. No one is punishing your body but you.

God does not hand you the extra five donuts out of the box and six pops during the day. The Holy Spirit is not forceful. Jesus said he was gentle and humble. Sometimes that puts us in a pickle. We let the sweet, quiet nature of Jesus get stamped down in our own willful rebellion. And our bodies are paying a terrible price. We are either overweight or too thin, we are exhausted, we are strung out on pop, coffee, cigarettes and drugs out the whazoo (prescriptions included!). Can't we just get back to being Goldie Locks, and get it just right? Balance and moderation. Do we even care to get there?

What about drinking alcohol? This can be a touchy subject for some Christians. We have freedom in Christ. The Bible says, "Do not get drunk on wine which leads to debauchery; instead be filled with the Spirit." Ephesians 5:18 To not drink to be drunk is the self-control we have been discussing for a good portion of the book. As a real "foodie," I see alcohol as part of a meal that compliments the food. I never look at alcohol as a fix for my problems or a means to getting drunk. Your call. To drink alcohol or not is up to you. Use your self-control and love for others in each social group to help you determine what the Holy Spirit would prefer you to do.

Kudos to you who are balanced in your bodies! Please find ways to help your sisters who are not. For those of you who want balance, you will need a dose of self-control, wisdom and some accountability. You must ask Jesus for some of his gentleness and humbleness. Why?

Because you need to be humble to ask someone to help you in this area of weakness with your body. You need to be gentle because you want to be mean and cast blame on those around you for your predicament.

Your beginning prayer is for God's wisdom and self-control. Wisdom for God to show you a true friend, someone who will be honest and uplifting as you travel down this road to regaining balance in your body. Self-control is needed in big doses, but it rarely comes that way. Small doses and small victories will lead to the balance you need. Gentleness and humbleness, the whole way!

Record your victories. Reward them with something other than the little demon that haunts you. If you are fighting weight, reward yourself with a new top that looks flattering instead of an extra cookie on Friday night! If you are fighting drugs or alcohol, reward yourself with a night out to a movie instead of hitting the bar or favorite smoking place.

So much help is out there. I don't need to go and list all the places in your town or city where you can get help. Get help through a Biblical counseling center if you don't have a loved one or trusted person to work with you. You can regain balance. I am rooting for you!

Our bodies need to be in the best shape possible to give our heart/soul and minds the receptacle they need to do their jobs to the best. It is the wholeness we cannot get away from. We are not exactly like a well-oiled machine working in a factory. We may have many working parts like the machine, Spirit-Mind-Body—but our machines need much more rest and care than a factory machine that can run 24/7 for weeks before needing maintenance. If we let ourselves go, sometimes the breakdown is devastating and may not be so easily repaired. Take a more balanced road and do care and maintenance regularly to avoid a serious crash.

Exercise

Not my favorite topic. I do exercise because I know it benefits my body and adds to my overall health. I am not a "gym rat" as one lady in my Bible study said about how much she loved working out. She loves being at the gym and sees herself as a little rat, slinking about using all the equipment with glee. Nope, not me. Have gym memberships, was a lifeguard and worked at our local pool, but not really into it. I work out for duty to bodily health. I'd prefer reading a good book. I must admit when I was young, I loved running 3-4 miles every day because it gave me the power to eat more junk food and never gain weight. Not the case anymore! Not really a balanced outlook on life!

Balance in exercise. Yes, we must do it. The Apostle Paul even uses examples of exercise symbolism in the letters he wrote. "For physical training is of some value, but godliness has value for all things, holding promise for both the present life and the life to come." 1 Timothy 4:8 Even Paul acknowledged physical training. They lived in the era of gladiators, Olympic games, and physical prowess of soldiers and warriors. It has value, but seeking to love God with your whole heart/soul, mind, strength and to love others has a greater, eternal value.

Paul said again, "Do you not know that in a race all the runners run, but only one gets the prize? Run in such a way as to get the prize. Everyone who competes in the games goes into strict training. They do it to get a crown that will not last, but we do it to get a crown that will last forever. Therefore, I do not run like someone running aimlessly; I do not fight like a boxer beating the air. No, I strike a blow to my body and make it my slave so that after I have preached to others, I myself will not be disqualified for the prize." 1 Corinthians 9:24-27

Paul knew his body carried around the good news of Jesus Christ. Our temple, our jar of clay with life giving water. He knew the health of his body would carry the good news of Jesus to more people if it were somewhat healthy vs. totally out of shape. How he treated his body would directly affect his ability and opportunity to share the good news of eternal life with others. Self-control and self-discipline are big themes in much of Paul's writings. Study and find out more.

What about your effectiveness as a witness of Jesus Christ when it comes to your body? It does make a difference. If others are looking at your out of shape, overweight or drug addicted body that is wheezing, shaking and turning blue at one step up into a coffee shop, do you think they will take you seriously that this Jesus guy can make a difference? You must get concerned that Jesus should be making a difference in your heart/soul, mind and body. You just can't accept some balance in one area and never work toward balance in the rest of your life.

Those of you who do have the fulness of healthy or intact physical body are exempt from some of this section. Your balance should be high in the spirit and mind and others will understand about the body. It's a no brainer. Your witness in balance of the heart/soul and mind will make up for any physical lack in the body. The Holy Spirit will see to it.

But you who are not all there physically…time to get exercising. Remember it has some value. You must get up and move. I understand about the desire to sit and read a good book for twelve hours straight! Or more like the Netflix marathon of Lord of the Rings…constant sitting and doing nothing is not too helpful for your body health.

What to do? Walking, biking, hiking, canoeing, kayaking, bowling, yoga, tai chi – you name it and you can find activities for one single person, doubles or team play. Exercise can be at home, at the gym or in nature. What is it that you find some joy and renewal in doing? Explore until you find something that will help keep your physical body active and in shape. Disclaimer here – check with your doctor before starting any physical activity if you have been inactive for a long time. You want to check with your health professional before starting on the exercise road if you have been sitting at a rest stop for a long time.

Your checkup will be a baseline for watching your heart rate and pulse rate during exercise. Start slow and sit down to rest if you feel like your heart is about to blow up or your lungs are on fire! Some of you will start with a five-minute walk in place in front of Netflix! Yeah! Keep going. Walk in place every day and make it longer each week. "Slow and steady wins the race," said the turtle to the hare.

Have some goals in mind for your body. Do you need to have a better heart rate? Are you needing to lose some pounds? Do you need to strengthen weak muscle tone? Focusing on one area will give you gains in all eventually. Pick the one goal that you feel would be the best for your witness as a follower of Jesus. Are you self-motivated or better with an accountability partner? Do you prefer gym, home, or nature? Get a pen and paper and write out a simple plan or goal for yourself if it will help you get going. Use self-control and self-discipline to get moving and keep moving.

Whatever you have decided to do; do it with all your heart (Colossians 3:10). God is for you getting healthy in your body. Be realistic and take it one day at a time. Reward yourself when you have met some of the mile markers on your goal path. A massage for sore muscles when you have run your first mile without stopping, a time in the sauna at the local gym for your first cycle class with only one stop! Exercise can be fun and rewarding, but it is a state that must come from your mind when your body hates to do it.

And for you, gym rats…you must balance exercise if it can too easily become a go to activity for you. You are the people who love running ten miles each day, will bike for 40 miles after work, will go rock climbing for days on end. Are you exercising so much that others in your life are getting neglected? God, Spouse, children, parents? Does God get any of your time? Do you read your Bible and spend time studying, meditating and contemplating God's word? In relation to the time you spend exercising, how much time are you spending with God and others? When physical exercise becomes an activity for self alone, you may have to adjust to find balance.

Start doing some of the exercises you like with others. The competition and company will keep you focused on others. Try doing exercises your spouse or kids like. Pick something you have never done and try it. Make a conscience effort to take the exercise off yourself and think on the benefits God and others should be looking at in your life. Are you physically getting in shape? Good. Are you clearer minded and able to sleep better? Great. Do others see your love of God motivating the care of your body? I hope so. Keep it balanced. Use self-control to stop too much exercise or change it up and refocus on God more if you realize it means more to you than Spirit and mind.

The real goal of body exercise should be that of staying healthy to share more of the good news of Jesus with others. The Apostle Paul uses the athletic symbolism so beautifully in this passage:

I want to know Christ—yes, to know the power of his resurrection and participation in his sufferings, becoming like him in his death, and so, somehow, attaining to the resurrection from the dead. Not that I have already obtained all this, or have already arrived at my goal, but I press on to take hold of that for which Christ Jesus took hold of me. Brothers and sisters, I do not consider myself yet to have taken hold of it. But one thing I do: Forgetting what is behind and straining toward what is ahead, I press on toward the goal to win the prize for which God has called me heavenward in Christ Jesus. All of us, then, who are mature should take such a view of things. And if on some point you think differently, that too God will make clear to you. Only let us live up to what we have already attained. Join together in following my example, brothers and sisters, and just as you have us as a model, keep your eyes on those who live as we do. For, as I have often told you before and now tell you again even with tears, many live as enemies of the cross of Christ. Their destiny is destruction, their god is their stomach, and their glory is in their shame. Their mind is set on earthly things. But our citizenship is in heaven. And we eagerly await a Savior from there, the Lord Jesus Christ, who, by the power that enables him to bring everything under his control, will transform our lowly bodies so that they will be like his glorious body." Philippians 3:10-21

Our goal is to share the good news of the eternal life, we have been gifted, with others. They need to know there is more. Even the most supreme athlete has a lowly body that can perish or become injured and useless with disease or an accident. But our heart/soul, mind and body together under the joyous relationship of knowing Jesus will see eternal life. Others need to know. The Beautiful Balance continues…

Outward Appearance

I will cover some 'touchy' areas for some of you in this section. Our outward appearance covers things like personal hygiene, clothing choices, beauty enhancement such as make up, hair color, hairstyles, and the dreaded topic of plastic surgery, piercings and tattoos.

Let me remind you of the Apostle Paul's tips, "All things are permissible, but not all things are beneficial, all things are lawful but not all things are helpful." We have a lot of freedom in Christ to care for and do outward effects on our bodies. Prayer, discernment and seeking wisdom from God might be something you want to undertake before getting extreme in any of the areas of outward appearance.

My go to lady in scripture is Queen Esther. You can read her entire story in the book of the Bible titled by her name, Esther. Esther was a sweet and obedient Jewish girl named Hadassah. She had been orphaned and was raised by her cousin Mordecai. When an edict went forth for a search to begin for a new queen in the great empire of Persia, her uncle sent her over to the royal palace to be considered for the queenly position.

Esther underwent twelve months of beauty treatments. Six months with oil and myrrh and six months with perfumes and cosmetics. There you go. The Bible's story on the delicate matter of outward beauty. Vanity is not just about the abuse of outward appearance, it is a trait that can have benefit or detriment. Vanity that is beneficial can gain a queenly title and be used by God to do the miracle of saving a whole people group for it, like in Esther's case. Or vanity can be a detrimental attitude of the heart that is constantly drawing attention to self and away from God. Esther's beauty treatments had some benefit along with her natural personality that drew people to her, like her caregiver eunuch and eventually the King. She was chosen as the new queen for the empire of Persia and used her position to save her entire Jewish nation from destruction. I love the story. Women in that day and age had very little influence and God in his amazing wisdom used the outward beauty of an obedient girl to save his people. Go God! Thanks, for one up on women!

I probably haven't put twelve months of beauty care into myself in my whole 50 years on earth! I have some vanity though. Enough to get up and shower each day, color my hair because my husband doesn't like it gray, style my hair, wear make-up, maybe paint my nails occasionally, get a pedi or manicure, etc. My list is going to be very different from yours.

Let's remember that we are daughters of King Jesus. Princesses in Christ's holy nation that are called out of darkness and into his wonderful light. (1 Peter 2:9) Princesses are queens in the making. Some vanity for King Jesus is to be expected. Do royal persons walk around in rags with filthy faces? I think not. Putting some effort into your royal appearance is a good way to keep up the maintenance of our Temple. Remember, we house the Holy Spirit, a royal gift indeed to carry around in our bodies.

Balance, you knew I would go there. We must balance our outward appearance with what the scriptures call a gentle and quiet spirit. The Apostle Peter writes:

> Your beauty should not come from outward adornment, such as elaborate hairstyles and the wearing of gold jewelry or fine clothes. Rather, it should be that of your inner self, the unfading beauty of a gentle and quiet spirit, which is of great worth in God's sight. For this is the way the holy women of the past who put their hope in God used to adorn themselves. 1 Peter 3:3-5

How do you balance this concept of a gentle and quiet inward self, loving God deeply and loving others with some outward beauty and care? This is a very personal area for all people. Some of what you will be comfortable with will have to do with your upbringing and culture.

For instance, in my area of Pennsylvania, you see many Amish and Mennonite ladies. Their culture and church practice would insist on wearing dresses, head coverings, no makeup, no hair color, no nail painting and no jewelry wearing. Plain. That is how their culture brings out the gentle and quiet spirit; by being purposely plain on the outside.

Most of us would shy away from being so plain and wall-flower like. Remember ladies, we are balanced in Christ and can go further with our outward appearance if it is part of our culture and not too attention getting. Modesty is a good word we can use here. We had a rule for our daughters, "no boob crack and no butt crack". The teen choices of clothing can leave little for the imagination and much for the young men to lust over. Keeping stylish with attire, but also finding a way to do it modestly says a lot about your inner character. Other people are looking closely at you. Are you thinking about reflecting Christ with your outward appearance? As my momma used to say, "Is Jesus some hussy street walker? Go get that off!" Being honest and accountable to each other as women is a good thing.

I must put a kudos up here for my husband and sons. They participated in being honest with us girls in the house and would honestly say if they thought any of our clothing was drawing too much attention in a sexual way. I appreciated that for myself and for my daughters.

It paid off as two of my sons have chosen beautiful wives who are both gentle and quiet spirits reflecting Christ and stylishly modest with their outward looks.

Where is your comfort level with your clothing? Have you ever had comments from others about your look? Too many whistles about tight pants or too much cleavage? Reflect on this. Make a balance assessment in this area if you need. Don't give me the, "I am an adult and can do what I want" lecture. You can, but is it helpful? Is it beneficial? Are others seeing Jesus in any outlandish clothing choices you might be making?

I told you this area was going to get annoying. We are looking to find purpose in God's greatest two commandments, but are we willing to assess and acquiesce and humble ourselves to make balance changes when we need?

Makeup, hair color, and jewelry are the same as clothing. Is it modest? I have a lot of free reign as a princess in God's kingdom here. I love crazy hair dye and crazy hairdos on other people. I have dyed and done crazy hair styles on all my kids, sons included! I keep it normal for myself.

Makeup is awesome as you get older. Need it for skin protection with the UV stuff in it and blending in all the ugly age spots! Jewelry is my bling, bling favorite! I do love matching jewelry that complements an outfit. Bracelets are my thing! I think this area is easy to assess and balance.

Plastic surgery, piercings and tattoos are another story. This area is getting into permanent outward body changes. Clothing, make-up, hair, and jewelry can be changed in a moment and tossed into the garbage if they aren't complimenting Christ or you. The big stuff of changing your body permanently needs prayer and mindful consideration before undertaking.

Plastic surgery is very personal, and most Christians just don't seem to want to discuss it. It is a no-brainer if you have had breast cancer and want to have a breast replacement. A woman's breasts are significant in who we are. The breast is beautiful and unique to women to serve as a way to arouse our husbands and feed our precious babies. It is part of our identity in God's creation of us. It is okay to want to keep up the outward appearance. It is just as okay to say goodbye to those cancer ridden breasts and never have a replacement if you don't want. Freedom to balance, I love Jesus for giving it to us.

What about getting new and bigger breasts just because you want it? Is it beneficial? Is it helpful? Will the size you desire make men lust after you? Will other women want to gouge their husband's eyes out when you walk in the room? Will other women turn their faces from you and avoid you because of it? Are you being honest with what you really want? Will you be glorifying Christ in the decision or just benefiting yourself and opening a can of worms you will regret? Think long and hard, pray and make Christ balanced decisions before doing anything permanent.

What if you have already done the breast surgery and all those questions I posed are a part of your life now? The change was permanent, you just can't easily go and have them taken out. You can change your attitude about your breasts. You can change your clothing to be more modest and cover up the cleavage you have been putting out there. You must desire to put the gentle and quiet spirit of a godly woman into and out of you. It needs to become more and the outward needs to become less. Not going to be easy.

The same will go for any other plastic surgery. Permanent is permanent. You just can't go back. Don't feel guilty if you want a nose job or ugly hair removed. Are you doing it to smooth out something that bothers you on the outside? Small changes can have a profound effect on a person if you were teased your whole life about it. Modern medicine is amazing, but don't abuse it. Your heart/soul, mind and body are one. Work on balancing your whole self, inside and out, in ways that will reflect your love of God and love toward others.

Piercings and tattoos are a subject some hate. We don't mind the regular pierced ear of a lady but go crazy with it and people freak! Tattoos – wow, this will be fun to discuss.

Again, helpful? Beneficial? Drawing more attention to you than pointing others to Christ? Hmmm… think on it before doing it. It will be permanent. The Old Testament has this verse, "'Do not cut your bodies for the dead or put tattoo marks on yourselves. I am the Lord." Leviticus 19:28 God wanted his people to be set apart from the other nations around them. All the others, were tattooed and cutting themselves with piercing of some sorts or other marks that ritualized religious practice God saw as detestable. God saw keeping yourself as you were created as beautiful enough.

I know the verse was meant for Jewish people under the law. It gave them clear direction from God to keep their mind and body on the path of holiness. We are under Christ's freedom. The old law is not part of us or our culture. However, the spirit of the law, the two greatest commandments are still at the forefront of our purpose. Are you loving God with your whole heart/soul, mind and body? Are you loving others like yourself? It puts a level of reflection and respect back on the Old Testament verse. Consider it deeply before getting a tattoo or piercing that is pulling you into what 'all others are doing'. God has called us to continue to be that holy nation, walking in holiness. Think on it.

I can't just tell you how to do this outward appearance thing. That is the freedom in Christ we have. It makes Christianity both beautiful and baffling. It is a heart/soul, mind and body thing. I can only share scripture verses for you to reflect on, wise attitude and behavior balance after the fact. Holiness is part of the miraculous change in balance Christ begins to make in our lives after we know him. It is internal and external because we are a whole being. We must think on reflecting Christ in our inward self and outward body.

Some of you will need to make balance changes in the outward appearance of your body. Some of you will be working on the attitude of heart and mind to reflect more clearly this love you have for God. Some of you will relish the new understanding of freedom you have from Christ about the care of your body. I am rooting for you as you grow in Beautiful Balance. So wonderful this purpose from God in his commandments! I am glad he gives us a lifetime to gain on holiness in our heart/soul, mind and body! "Finally, Be strong in the Lord and in his mighty power!" Ephesians 6:10. Reflect this love of God and command to love others with your body.

CHAPTER SEVEN

⟫⟫⟫ Loving Others ⟪⟪⟪

The second greatest command, love your neighbor like yourself. Kind of a weird way of saying love others. Jesus knew, though, that it would be impossible to love someone as much or better than you loved yourself unless loving God had come first. We don't have any problem loving ourselves. We love ourselves too much, really. If we could easily love others as much as we love ourselves, Jesus wouldn't have made it a command to love your neighbor like yourself. We must work at this. That is why the first part of the command came before this...truly loving God with our whole heart/soul, mind and body gives us the supernatural ability through the Holy Spirit to put others above ourselves on the love scale.

Beautiful Balance makes you think of a scale. Others are usually lacking in the amount of love we give to ourselves vs. love we give to others. Some of you will claim a martyrdom of love sacrifice here. Mothers will claim how much they love and sacrifice for their families. Yes, I know. But so often you have your own agenda and you have become an expert at letting others think you are loving others when really you are getting something you want. OH, that hurts to see ourselves as selfish!

Jesus compared us to generally evil people in his little parables.

> "Ask and it will be given to you; seek and you will find; knock and the door will be opened to you. For every-one who asks receives; the one who seeks finds; and to the one who knocks, the door will be opened. "Which of you, if your son asks for bread, will give him a stone?

Or if he asks for a fish, will give him a snake? If you, then, though you are evil, know how to give good gifts to your children, how much more will your Father in heaven give good gifts to those who ask him! So in everything, do to others what you would have them do to you, for this sums up the Law and the Prophets." Matthew 7:7-12

Even evil people can do good to others. So, what then is the stuff we should be asking God for in the parable? A relationship with him, to love him with your whole heart/soul, mind and body; so then, your ability to do to others what you would have them do to you becomes supernatural. Something other than ourselves. Something where love is an attitude and action, putting others above ourselves in care, respect and sacrifice.

So much of our scripture is filled with how people loved others. It is easiest to follow the example of others from God's word in how love action will look in our own lives. Jesus took the love action to greatest degree. He came knowing he would sacrifice himself so the rest of us would not have to. Jesus is the love sacrifice that took our place. He willingly gave his life so that everyone who believes on him will have eternal life. Their sin gone and wiped clean with his blood sacrifice.

> *Greater love has no one than this: to lay down one's life for one's friends.*
>
> *John 15:13 (NIV)*

There are many and have been many over the years of history who have given their life that another may live. Parents and war heroes have sacrificed themselves for their children and others. It is the most poignant picture of sacrificial love. Jesus said, "Greater love has no one than this: to lay down one's life for one's friends" John 15:13. Jesus laid down his life for all that would follow him, he calls us friends. "You are my friends if you do what I command. I no longer call you servants, because a servant does not know his master's business. Instead,

I have called you friends, for everything that I learned from my Father I have made known to you." John 15:14-15

Not many will have to give love an action of sacrifice that results in the death of someone in exchange for the life of another. Most of us will spend the rest of our lives reading the Bible, studying and meditating on the love actions of others and figuring out how to apply that knowledge into a real love action for our own lives. You do so many love actions a day you don't even realize it. A kind word to someone, making a meal for your family, doing the dishes, finishing laundry, a smile to someone, a hand with groceries, or better yet – giving someone your place in line at the grocery store. Love is seen so often we sometimes grow cold to it happening around us.

That is the question I am asked most often: What does loving your neighbor like yourself look like? It looks like a nice chicken dinner you just slaved over and put on the table for your family. You did your cooking and slaving out of love, even though some days it feels like a drudgery. Attitude is more important in expressing love than the action. How was your attitude when that dinner was served? Did you expect praise and kudos all around for your effort? Or did you pray over each part of the meal as you prepared it and ask God's blessing to go into each person who would partake of the nourishment you just prepared? Hmmm... the attitude can make all the difference. Even if some family members turned their noses up at the meal, you can rest in your love of God and your love you put into the action. And you can tell little whiner child their plate will be in the fridge to eat later!

Smiles, and a good sense of humor, along with having no expectations of others can help you keep an attitude of love. You can control your attitude. You cannot control others' attitudes. Having thin skin and taking things personal is not going to help in gaining an attitude of love. You can't always know what someone else is feeling or why they might have reacted in a mean way toward you. It could be that they just had bad news or a long list of unknowns.

"May the God who gives endurance and encouragement give you the same **attitude** of mind toward each other that Christ

Jesus had." Romans 15:5 Here comes the wholeness again. We must have our minds engaged in this attitude thing. Love is not just an action we can easily enjoy doing with our bodies. Jesus's attitude toward us was love, love and more love. We can discipline our minds to have an attitude of love. That is good news because I don't always feel like I love others well!

I will share an example. I really feel ignorant sharing this, but it was an experience I learned from. I had been doing some ministry with very poor and special needs people. My body did the actions of helping, cleaning, taking them to the store, etc. But some days my head and heart were not into the love. I was struggling with their body odor, for they were not clean. I was struggling with their language, for they spoke in more curse words than I had heard in years. I was struggling with the filth with which they surrounded themselves. Not too loving on my part.

They never knew, actually no one knew how I was feeling except God. I kept going on and confessed in my heart my lack of love and asked God for more compassion. So, the action of doing love was visible to them and eventually did make a difference, but the attitude of love wavered from low to high according to my self-control and discipline from God. Only my supernatural relationship with loving God wholly, transposed itself into following the command to love others even when I didn't have the right attitude.

It is a command – to love others like yourself, to love your neighbor supernaturally! It can be easy to do the love in the beginning, but harder to have the attitude of love as time goes on. Any married couple can attest to that. The honeymoon, google-eyed stuff eventually wears off and the actions of love continue, but sometimes the attitude slips a little. After one hundred thousand dinners served, sometimes the attitude slacks and the plates get slapped down on the table a little hard.

I like Ephesians 4:23 to help me focus on the right attitude. "Be made new in the attitude of your minds." The entire rest of the chapter takes time to give examples of this renewed attitude of mind that is like Christ. Read through it now:

Be made new in the attitude of your minds and to

put on the new self, created to be like God in true **righteousness and holiness.** Therefore each of you must put off falsehood and **speak truthfully to your neighbor**, for we are all members of one body. "In your anger do not sin": Do not let the sun go down while you are still angry, and do not give the devil a foothold. Anyone who has been stealing **must steal no longer**, but must work, **doing something useful** with their own hands, that they may have something to **share with those in need**. Do not let any **unwholesome talk come out of your mouths**, but only **what is helpful** for building others up according to their needs, that it may benefit those who listen. And do not grieve the Holy Spirit of God, with whom you were sealed for the day of redemption. **Get rid of all bitterness, rage and anger, brawling and slander, along with every form of malice. Be kind and compassionate to one another, forgiving each other, just as in Christ God forgave you.** Ephesians 4:23-32 (author's bold print added)

I bolded some of the actions and attitudes. Put on a new self. How on earth does that happen? By attitude — knowing the truth of who you are in Jesus and knowing that you have his righteousness and holiness. It is a symbolic picture of what Jesus does for us and how the Holy Spirit works in us. I haven't seen any holiness suits on sale at the local Christian book store. Hint: You find out the truths Jesus wants you to put on in the Bible. You must read it and study it to grasp the ability to have the attitude to put on that new self.

Speak truthfully. Well, that is a simple virtue to speak truthfully. No lying, honesty that all people appreciate. That is one of our love things that can be done by action. Using your mouth to speak truth. Your heart and mind must grasp the attitude that speaking truthfully is of the same mind as Christ.

Don't steal. That is also one of the ten commandments. Good idea. Stealing is against man's law and it is against God. It involves an action, but also an attitude. Jesus wants the person who has been stealing to do something useful and helpful instead. There is the action of putting on a new self that doesn't steal any longer, but instead helps others.

No unwholesome talk. This is what we want to take off. It could include things like gossip, slander, swearing and cussing, and coarse joking. And the new self should be putting on beneficial or encouraging talk. That could include things like kindness, courtesy, pump me up coach talk! Attitude is making all the difference in loving others as we want to be loved!

Dump the anger, bitterness, rage, and malice of any sort. Put on kindness, compassion, and forgiveness. I did that in my ministry to those poverty-stricken folks. I had to clear the junk and make the real effort to put on the right stuff. I was very aware it was in me, and the Holy Spirit gave me aide to get the new me together.

There you have it. A mini Bible study just for you. What did you think? I bet you didn't even realize you were studying God's word as I wrote those paragraphs. The scriptures are full of wonderful examples of love in action and love in attitude. You need to read your Bible. There are four books just written on the account of Jesus life and how he walked in a love that gave action and attitude together. The gospels of Matthew, Mark, Luke and John are wonderful. I suggest a red-letter version of the Bible while reading through these books. The red lettering highlights actual words of Jesus and they can become a great encouragement.

Jesus did do some awesome 'Son of God' stuff like healing people, walking on water, feeding five thousand with a few loaves of bread and little fish, and raising the dead. Cool, he was God in the Flesh and it would have made sense to show a little power while he was here. But remember, he has left us his Holy Spirit to continue the work. No, we will probably not go around doing 'Son of God' miracles, but we can go around loving others in action and attitude like Jesus.

Church lingo says we should be the 'hands and feet of Jesus'. We are his witnesses and those who do the love in action and attitude until he returns from heaven. Each small thing we do in Jesus' name is putting to action and attitude with our spirit, mind and bodies what he has designed for us.

The Attitude and Action

Here is where some of the finding your purposes in the greatest two commandments comes in. You love God through Jesus. You are gaining more and more love for God each day through the power of the Holy Spirit. You are getting what it means to love God with your whole heart/soul, mind and strength. You are doing love to others every day.

Your purpose in the two greatest commands has just become clearer. You must increase in this attitude and action of love each day. Jesus becomes more, and you become less. You have put him on and you are not taking him off. The Apostle Paul says in Galatians, "for all of you who were baptized into Christ have clothed yourselves with Christ." Galatians 3:27 and because we have done that we can, "Therefore, as God's chosen people, holy and dearly loved, clothe yourselves with compassion, kindness, humility, gentleness and patience." Galatians 3:12. This verse combines, the actions of love with the attitude of love.

for all of you who were baptized into Christ have clothed yourselves with Christ. Galatians 3:27 (NIV)

Some of those spiritual fruits listed in Ephesians Paul also lists in Galatians 5:22-23 "But the fruit of the Spirit is love, joy, peace, patience, kindness, goodness, faithfulness, gentleness, and self-control." These are things that can have an action of love associated with it or an attitude of love in how you go about your daily life. These are the new you, things you can put on in the attitude of your mind to be like Jesus. Your new set of clothes, tailor-made by Jesus, and put on by the Holy Spirit living in you.

Your purpose is tailor-made by Jesus living in you. Every person will carry out the action and attitude of kindness very differently from day to day. And the same for each new piece of the garments of holiness Jesus has been working on in your heart. Old clothes and attitudes and actions are being tossed. New clothes are in the making. I like the picture and I like what I am seeing in the mirror. Jesus is covering me with tailor-made holiness garments vs the pathetic choices of garments I have been wearing. That is good news and a great path of purpose. Praise God, the purpose is being created by his power in me!

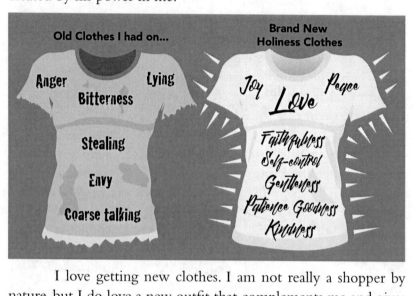

I love getting new clothes. I am not really a shopper by nature, but I do love a new outfit that complements me and gives me a new attitude for a date with the hubby. The clothes Jesus has for me are part of a complete package of holiness. Much better than the newest fad outfit I can offer my hubby. God is so wonderful in setting our purposes out in such a way we can begin to see them and discover them for ourselves.

All these new garments that will cover me in holiness are going to be worked out through my personality, the place God has put me, and specific good works and plans he has set aside for me to do. You have a different list, agenda, and purpose. So wonderful! Each person will be part of God's big picture of bringing glory to himself and spreading the good news of Jesus throughout the whole earth. Gives me goosebumps to think that big! What I do, what you do each day is important to God and fulfills our purpose in loving him with our whole heart/soul, mind, body and loving others like ourselves.

Jesus was holiness in perfect purity and completely sinless. His holiness flowed out through his service or acts of love toward others. The miracles, teachings and life examples of this are the legacy we must study, apply and try. Jesus said, "For even the Son of Man did not come to be served, but to serve, and to give his life as a ransom for many." Mark 10:45. Jesus served God and others in love. He lived out the greatest two commandments in love actions and love attitudes. Jesus' holiness is imparted to us through the gift of his Holy Spirit.

One of my favorite life verses I have chosen from the Bible speaks about this greater purpose of service and love from God. "We are God's workmanship, created in Christ Jesus, to do good works, which God himself prepared in advance for us to do." Ephesians 2:10. No mistakes with God. Workmanship implies an artisan creating the perfect work of beauty and eyecatching results. We are in God through Jesus, and the Holy Spirit confirms this in our heart. Good works are already lined up for me to do. Wow! That takes some pressure off. My service is needed, and I will work at my good works with love.

If today you are getting up and changing the baby's diaper at 5 AM, then groggily heading down to prepare breakfast for the hubby and rest of the little hoard that needs to get on the school bus by 6:30, you are surely doing a good work God had prepared for you. You are a servant with an opportunity to serve in love.

If you are driving to work on the freeway singing praise songs to God on your way to work, you are doing a good work God prepared for you. You are a servant, with an opportunity to serve in love.

If you are seeking intently for more guidance and direction from God about other good works you don't know about yet, you are surely doing a good work from God. You are a servant with an opportunity to serve in love.

Living your life in the greatest two commandments of loving God and loving others while working out the change of garments from the old you to the new you can happen with the balance Christ offers. It is God's purposes working in us, transforming us. Perfections, directions and the vast knowledge of the

truth being poured into you from the scriptures will give refine-
ment to your new garments. The purpose tailor is at work and
Christ gives the balance during the fitting. You can walk with balance in God's purposes. The new you will look for opportunities
to love God and others. You will begin to see God tailoring those
new garments with perfect balance in Christ.

Our specific ways to become the servant of love in life are
already laid out by God. Some of us administer, some help, some
preach, some teach. Whatever we do, our purpose is to do that
with a servant heart like Jesus and to serve in love. This is so beautiful, this balance we find in Christ. We should be excited to get
up tomorrow and do this love thing with a whole new attitude!
I'm excited, I hope you are too! Each new day is another chance
to love in attitude and action, and to become Beautifully Balanced.

It takes a lifetime to love God with your whole heart/soul,
mind and body and to love others like yourself. Continue your
journey of finding purpose in the two greatest commandments
from God. I am traveling on the road with you. You are letting
Christ transform you and take off your old garments and renew
and refresh you with new garments. Old to new – a Beautiful
Balance benefit!

CHAPTER EIGHT

ꜱꜱꜱ Final Thoughts on ꜱꜱꜱ Beautiful Balance

Some final thoughts as I close this first book. We have journeyed through the main themes of Beautiful Balance: Spirit, Mind, Body. Each part in perfect unity with the whole. Our purpose is to live out the two greatest commandments that give us Beautiful Balance. We love God with our whole being, spirit, mind, and body and we love others like ourselves. God has given us all we need to have Beautiful Balance.

The balance begins and remains always with Christ at the center, holding us steady as we gain understanding and begin our spiritual journey. A relationship with Jesus gives us the heart and soul beginning to our Spiritual balance. Our spirits recognize God, call out to God and desire to be one with him. Our spiritual nature connects with God because he is Spirit.

The overwhelming emotions, the heart and soul, the very spiritual nature of ourselves has been given the expectant emotion of hope. Hope calls out to Christ. Hope is Christ. We know God is there through the hope of Jesus. To love God now is very much in our grasp.

We are continously cultivating the Beautiful Balance of the Spirit, Mind and Body.

Jesus remains the fulcrum of the balance, always bringing us back to him to have self-control and peace in our minds and our bodies. Our relationship with Jesus grows each day he blesses us with understanding in our minds and the reality that we can love God wholly and love others like ourselves.

Our minds are the amazing power house given by God. Knowledge, understanding, and the very secrets of life are given in God's word and our minds can access all of it. Our minds are the piece of the Beautiful Balance puzzle that make the daily victories of love possible. We can know God and be known by God. The relationship with Christ is solidified in our minds.

Our minds pursue the body into creating love attitudes and love actions. This of course, is the supernatural work of Jesus in our lives. We care for our bodies to keep the mind alive and the spirit vibrant. We begin to understand the love attitude toward God more and more and we make it into a real and tangible love action when we connect with others. The Balance is Beautiful.

We are continuously cultivating the Beautiful Balance of the Spirit, Mind and Body. Love is the thread that connects our spirits, minds and bodies to God through Jesus and connects us to others. It is the two commands. It is the love of God toward us that draws us in. When we are filled with it, we give it to others. The picture is of pure joy.

Joy is love on steroids. It is a blessing we receive from the Beautiful Balance of finding our purpose from God in loving him and loving others. Joy is a steady love that is based in our relationship with Christ. Joy flows from God and back out through us. It fills us, overflows to others and cannot be stolen.

I will leave you with that final word: JOY! I invite you to learn more about JOY in the short Bible study I have included traveling through the book of Philippians – the letter of Joy! Joy is part of the Beautiful Balance, find it, share it! **Journey to Joy with me**...

Resources

Grace for the Afflicted, Matthew Stanford, Intervarsity Press, 2008 Boundaries, Henry Cloud, Zondervan, 1992

Battlefield of the Mind, Joyce Meyer, FaithWords, 1995

Practicing the Presence of God, Brother Lawrence

Toxic Thoughts, Caroline Leaf, ChurchMedia, 2017

ꯁꯗ Philippians: Journey to Joy ꯁꯗ

I suggest doing this Bible study in a small group of about 4-6 people. Make time to meet once a week for about 1-2 hours. Concentrate on one chapter a week or a portion of a chapter.

WEEK 1

Paul was the writer of Philippians in our Bible. He was a Jew and turned to Christ on the road to Damascus (Acts 9). Prior to knowing Jesus, he was also at the death of the first Christian martyr, Stephen. We see Stephen's death in Acts 7 and 8. Acts 7:58 reads, "Meanwhile the witnesses laid their coats at the feet of a young man named Saul." Acts 8:1 says, "And Saul approved of their killing him."

Read Acts 9 and discuss this account of Paul's conversion to Christ.

Saul's Conversion Acts 9:1-25

1 Meanwhile, Saul was still breathing out murderous threats against the Lord's disciples. He went to the high priest 2 and asked him for letters to the synagogues in Damascus, so that if he found any there who belonged to the Way, whether men or women, he might take them as prisoners to Jerusalem. 3 As he neared Damascus on his journey, suddenly a light from heaven flashed around him. 4 He fell to the ground and heard a voice say to him, "Saul, Saul, why do you persecute me?"

5 "Who are you, Lord?" Saul asked.

"I am Jesus, whom you are persecuting," he replied. 6 "Now get up and go into the city, and you will be told what you must do."

7 The men traveling with Saul stood there speechless; they

heard the sound but did not see anyone. 8 Saul got up from the ground, but when he opened his eyes he could see nothing. So they led him by the hand into Damascus. 9 For three days he was blind, and did not eat or drink anything.

10 In Damascus there was a disciple named Ananias. The Lord called to him in a vision, "Ananias!"

"Yes, Lord," he answered.

11 The Lord told him, "Go to the house of Judas on Straight Street and ask for a man from Tarsus named Saul, for he is praying. 12 In a vision he has seen a man named Ananias come and place his hands on him to restore his sight."

13 "Lord," Ananias answered, "I have heard many reports about this man and all the harm he has done to your holy people in Jerusalem.

14 And he has come here with authority from the chief priests to arrest all who call on your name."

15 But the Lord said to Ananias, "Go! This man is my chosen instrument to proclaim my name to the Gentiles and their kings and to the people of Israel. 16 I will show him how much he must suffer for my name."

17 Then Ananias went to the house and entered it. Placing his hands on Saul, he said, "Brother Saul, the Lord—Jesus, who appeared to you on the road as you were coming here—has sent me so that you may see again and be filled with the Holy Spirit." 18 Immediately, something like scales fell from Saul's eyes, and he could see again. He got up and was baptized, 19 and after taking some food, he regained his strength.

Saul spent several days with the disciples in Damascus. 20 At once he began to preach in the synagogues that Jesus is the Son of God. 21 All those who heard him were astonished and asked, "Isn't he the man who raised havoc in Jerusalem among those who call on this name? And hasn't he come here to take them as prisoners to the chief priests?" 22 Yet Saul grew more and more powerful and baffled the Jews living in Damascus by proving that Jesus is the Messiah.

23 After many days had gone by, there was a conspiracy among the Jews to kill him, 24 but Saul learned of their plan. Day

and night they kept close watch on the city gates in order to kill him. 25 But his followers took him by night and lowered him in a basket through an opening in the wall.

1. How has Christ worked in your life?

2. Share your story of how you came to know Christ. Or your continued search if you are still seeking spiritual answers.

3. Are you seeing the Holy Spirit making Christ visible?

4. Can you sense the beginning of Paul's spiritual joy in his salvation?

WEEK 2

Paul was the writer of the letter or book in our Bible. He was a Jew and turned to Christ on the road to Damascus (Acts 9). Last week we read his conversion account and discussed it. Paul arrived in Philippi on his second missionary journey (Acts 16) and started the new church with the first European follower of Christ, Lydia, a businesswoman. Take a few minutes to read Acts chapter 16.

Paul came to Derbe and then to Lystra, where a disciple named Timothy lived, whose mother was Jewish and a believer but whose father was a Greek. 2 The believers at Lystra and Iconium spoke well of him. 3 Paul wanted to take him along on the journey, so he circumcised him because of the Jews who lived in that area, for they all knew that his father was a Greek. 4 As they traveled from town to town, they delivered the decisions reached by the apostles and elders in Jerusalem for the people to obey. 5 So the churches were strengthened in the faith and grew daily in numbers.6 Paul and his companions traveled throughout the region of Phrygia and Galatia, having been kept by the Holy Spirit from preaching the word in the province of Asia. 7 When they came to the border of Mysia, they tried to enter Bithynia, but the Spirit of Jesus would not allow them to. 8 So they passed by Mysia and went down to Troas. 9 During the night Paul had a vision of a man of Macedonia standing and begging him, "Come over to Macedonia and help us." 10 After Paul had seen the vision, we got ready at once to leave for Macedonia, concluding that God had called us to preach the gospel to them.11 From Troas we put out to sea and sailed straight for Samothrace, and the next day we went on to Neapolis. 12 From there we traveled to Philippi, a Roman colony and the leading city of that district of Macedonia. And we stayed there several days.

13 On the Sabbath we went outside the city gate to the river, where we expected to find a place of prayer. We sat down and began to speak to the women who had gathered there. 14 One of those listening was a woman from the city of Thyatira named Lydia, a dealer in purple cloth. She was a worshiper of God. The Lord opened her heart to respond to Paul's message. 15 When

she and the members of her household were baptized, she invited us to her home. "If you consider me a believer in the Lord," she said, "come and stay at my house." And she persuaded us.

16 Once when we were going to the place of prayer, we were met by a female slave who had a spirit by which she predicted the future. She earned a great deal of money for her owners by fortune-telling. 17 She followed Paul and the rest of us, shouting, "These men are servants of the Most High God, who are telling you the way to be saved." 18 She kept this up for many days. Finally Paul became so annoyed that he turned around and said to the spirit, "In the name of Jesus Christ I command you to come out of her!" At that moment the spirit left her.

19 When her owners realized that their hope of making money was gone, they seized Paul and Silas and dragged them into the marketplace to face the authorities. 20 They brought them before the magistrates and said, "These men are Jews, and are throwing our city into an uproar. 21 by advocating customs unlawful for us Romans to accept or practice."

22 The crowd joined in the attack against Paul and Silas, and the magistrates ordered them to be stripped and beaten with rods. 23 After they had been severely flogged, they were thrown into prison, and the jailer was commanded to guard them carefully. 24 When he received these orders, he put them in the inner cell and fastened their feet in the stocks.

25 About midnight Paul and Silas were praying and singing hymns to God, and the other prisoners were listening to them. 26 Suddenly there was such a violent earthquake that the foundations of the prison were shaken. At once all the prison doors flew open, and everyone's chains came loose. 27 The jailer woke up, and when he saw the prison doors open, he drew his sword and was about to kill himself because he thought the prisoners had escaped. 28 But Paul shouted, "Don't harm yourself! We are all here!"

29 The jailer called for lights, rushed in and fell trembling before Paul and Silas. 30 He then brought them out and asked, "Sirs, what must I do to be saved?"

31 They replied, "Believe in the Lord Jesus, and you will be saved—you and your household." 32 Then they spoke the word of

the Lord to him and to all the others in his house. 33 At that hour of the night the jailer took them and washed their wounds; then immediately he and all his household were baptized. 34 The jailer brought them into his house and set a meal before them; he was filled with joy because he had come to believe in God—he and his whole household.

35 When it was daylight, the magistrates sent their officers to the jailer with the order: "Release those men." 36 The jailer told Paul, "The magistrates have ordered that you and Silas be released. Now you can leave. Go in peace."

37 But Paul said to the officers: "They beat us publicly without a trial, even though we are Roman citizens, and threw us into prison. And now do they want to get rid of us quietly? No! Let them come themselves and escort us out."

38 The officers reported this to the magistrates, and when they heard that Paul and Silas were Roman citizens, they were alarmed. 39 They came to appease them and escorted them from the prison, requesting them to leave the city. 40 After Paul and Silas came out of the prison, they went to Lydia's house, where they met with the brothers and sisters and encouraged them. Then they left."

Look at the beginnings of the new church at Philippi.

1. What are some of Lydia's gifts? Do you see how God worked through gifts she already had but now can use for God's glory?

2. Do you sense joy in your own life when you use your God given gifts and talents to love him, love others and walk in your purposes?

The change of old to new was significant for Paul, he changed his name from Saul, the old persecutor of Christians, to Paul, the new Christ follower and ambassador of Christ to the non-Jews or Gentiles of the world. Paul's name change is noted in Acts 13:9, right after he is beginning his first missionary journey and walking in the purpose God has for his life, to bring the good news to Gentiles.

1. If you are a Christian, have you ever thought about what name you might like to have if the custom of the day and culture encouraged you to do it?

2. Many cultures around the world do take on name changes to Bible characters names after they become Christians. Think on it.

3. What are some things you have been doing since Christ has called you his own?

Read through Philippians 1
JOY!
Paul has this theme of joy throughout the book. He is finding joy while in prison, writing this letter to the Philippian church. Joy comes through knowing Christ (Philippians 4:4)

1. What brings you joy?

2. Is joy a fleeting happiness or something deeper?

3. How can Paul feel and find joy in dire circumstances of being in prison?

4. Who is the source of Paul's joy?

5. Do you see joy as part of that new garment of holiness that makes you beautifully balanced in Christ?

Rejoice in the Lord always! Again, I say Rejoice!
Philippians 4:4 (NIV)

6. In verse 4, how do you pray with joy? Share some examples of how that might happen.

Take time to read the chapter again and underline verses that speak to you personally. Discuss your favorite verses in your group and share why those verses are calling out to you. What verses speak to you about your beautiful balance, the purpose to love God wholly and love others like yourself?

WEEK 3

Read through Philippians 2

We see snippets of joy again in chapter two.

1. How was Paul's hoping to see his joy completed? (verse 2-4)

2. Paul describes Christ's humility in verses 5-11. What did Christ's humility lead to?

3. Do you see humility as a way to secure more joy?

4. Could humility assist you in finding beautiful balance?

5. How could being more humble in your own life lead to more joy?

6. Why does Paul mention Timothy and Epaphroditus in verses 19-30?

7. What did each of them do, a love attitude and love action, that gave Paul more joy?

Paul makes it clear in verses 5–11 that:

Our beautiful balance in spirit:

8. What was a clear vision or purpose that God gave to Paul on the road to Damascus? (Acts 9)

9. Do you have a clear vision or purpose that God is working out in your life?

10. What are some ways you can seek or discover God's purposes in your life?

Again for this chapter, underline verses that the Holy Spirit is calling out to you. Share with your group about a specific verse that you used this past week in your life.

Share a story about someone in your life who brought more joy because of a love attitude or love action you experienced with them or from them.

WEEK 4

Begin by having the leader open in prayer.

Have someone or several take turns reading Philippians 3 aloud.

Paul takes a turn and mentions the body in the chapter.

1. What is circumcision? Is this necessary to become a wholly balanced follower of Jesus?

2. What does Paul consider garbage (look at verse 5-8)?

3. What is the prize we should be looking to gain (verse 9-10)?

4. Are the outward things we do to our body going to gain us Christ?

5. Reflecting on verse 21, what do you imagine your glorious body will be like when you get to heaven with Christ?

6. Are we just body? Do you see the spirit, mind and body working together to gain the prize?

WEEK 5

Begin by opening in prayer. Read Philippians 4 aloud.

Paul shows joy in the beautiful balance of the mind in chapter four:

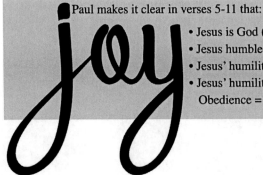

Paul makes it clear in verses 5-11 that:

- Jesus is God (verse 6)
- Jesus humbled himself (verse 7-8)
- Jesus' humility led to sacrifice (verse 8)
- Jesus' humility was in obedience to God. Obedience = Exalted Kingship (verse 9)

Take the time to read through the chapter again and underline the verses that speak to you personally.

You can choose to be joyful. God has already given the blessing of joy through our relationship with him. Joy can be called up as part of our Beautiful Balance through our mind.

1. What are some things you do to bring joy up, so you can sense it? Review the list above and talk about what Paul did to bring up his joy.

2. Do you rejoice in the concern you have for others?

3. Does your concern motivate you to take love action and do something?

4. What is Paul's secret of contentment?

5. Share a story of when you had very little and felt content?

6. Share about a time of plenty. Did you feel motivated to give more to others in your time of plenty?

WEEK 6

Philippians Review

Paul's Beautiful Balance in spirit:

Paul counts everything loss and garbage from his past except the new spiritual relationship he began with Christ (chapter 3, verses 7-11)

Is your relationship with God in balance through Christ?

Do you need to confess Jesus Christ as Lord and Savior and bow humbly before the King of the Universe, who alone can forgive sins and make you spiritually whole? (Chapter 2:5-11)

Paul's Beautiful Balance in the mind:

Paul challenges us to be joyful in having the mind of Christ (chapter 2).

1. Are you disciplining your mind to bring joy to the surface of your thoughts?

2. Is your mind pushing your body to begin to act in joy, or give love action toward others?

Paul's Beautiful Balance in the body:

1. Are you using your body as the conduit for joy by loving others?

2. Have you physically helped someone with your body? That includes kind talk (our lips give service to what our mind wants to speak)! Or carried something for them? Or built something for them...

Study Suggestions:

Choose the verses that spoke to you and you underlined and begin to memorize them. Write them on your phone note pad, or use small note cards to keep in your wallet or purse. Keep it simple, maybe one or two verses per chapter. Give yourself time, weeks to memorize. Bring joy up each time you reflect and practice your verses.

My suggested memory verses are in the following table. Copy the page onto cardstock and have your own set of verses handy. Or take a photo of the chart on your cell phone and refer to it often to help you memorize joy filled Beautifully Balanced scripture.

"In all my prayers for you, I always pray with joy." Philippians 1:4	"And this is my prayer: that your love may abound more and more in knowledge and depth of insight, so that you may be able to discern what is best and may be pure and blameless for the day of Christ, filled with the fruit of righteousness that comes through Jesus Christ—to the glory and praise of God" Philippians 1:9-11	"then make my joy complete by being likeminded, having the same love, being one in spirit and of one mind." Philippians 2:2
"Do nothing out of selfish ambition or vain conceit. Rather, in humility value others above yourselves, not looking to your own interests but each of you to the interests of the others." Philippians 2:3-4	"Do everything without grumbling or arguing." Philippians 2:14	"Further, my brothers and sisters, rejoice in the Lord!" Philippians 3:1
"What is more, I consider everything a loss because of the surpassing worth of knowing Christ Jesus my Lord, for whose sake I have lost all things. I consider them garbage, that I may gain Christ." Philippians 3:8	"I press on toward the goal to win the prize for which God has called me heavenward in Christ Jesus." Philippians 3:14	"Rejoice in the Lord always. I will say it again: Rejoice!" Philippians 4:4
"Do not be anxious about anything, but in every situation, by prayer and petition, with thanksgiving, present your requests to God. And the peace of God, which transcends all understanding, will guard your hearts and your minds in Christ Jesus." Philippians 4:6-7	"Finally, brothers and sisters, whatever is true, whatever is noble, whatever is right, whatever is pure, whatever is lovely, whatever is admirable —if anything is excellent or praiseworthy— think about such things. Whatever you have learned or received or heard from me, or seen in me—put it into practice. And the God of peace will be with you." Philippians 4:8-9	"I have learned to be content whatever the circumstances. I know what it is to be in need, and I know what it is to have plenty. I have learned the secret of being content in any and every situation, whether well fed or hungry, whether living in plenty or in want. I can do all this through him who gives me strength." Philippians 4:11-13

About the Author

You will find me, most often, in my favorite place-sipping hot tea, Bible and journal in hand, on my porch soaking in the view of the beautiful Pennsylvania farm land surrounding my home. On that porch, I love to sit and have deep conversation about God's purposes in our lives with family and friends and how the love of God spurs us on to accomplish his work. From those conversations and time spent in God's word, I write my daily devotions and create notes for upcoming books and other written works God has in my heart. Become a part of the conversation and join me by following my Beautiful Balance Facebook page: https://www.facebook.com/BBwisdom/

There you can follow my book signings and speaking engagements schedule and find daily Beautiful Balance wisdom from God's word.

Acknowledgments

I know authors sometimes wonder where to start when it comes to giving out a thank-you for their book. I will start right with Cohort 94 at Geneva College. I was in my third class, communications, working toward my master's in organizational leadership, when I received an 'aha' moment and serious challenge from Dr. Maureen Vanterpool. She challenged me and said, "Ellen, if you don't get on the bus, you are going to be left in the dust." That statement was meant for me to rise to the occasion and learn how to use technology in a sufficient manner and to personally engage in using my writing and speaking skills more. I got on the bus.

I prepared a mission trip for my sister and me to Romania and spoke at a three-day ladies' conference on our school break that summer. God racked my brain on that trip and gave me the idea for Beautiful Balance. It started out as a women's newsletter for church and very quickly I began writing notes to myself about putting a book together. So, thank you, Dr. Vanterpool, for challenging me and pouring yourself into each one of us in Cohort 94!

To the rest of my professors at Geneva and cohort 94, thanks for the encouragement and thought-provoking challenges. Dr. Stanko, a big thank you for publishing with Urban Press. I am grateful.

The second big thank you goes to Regina Johnson. Regina was my partner at the ladies Bible study and support for creating all the graphics of the first newsletter. Regina is an awesome graphic designer and knew just what I was looking for each time I wanted pictures to enhance my words. She has stuck with me all through those early stages and into the birth of the book. Thanks, Regina, you are the best!

The third thank you goes to all the ladies who sat under me and Regina. Your transparent hearts in loving God and loving others inspired much of Beautiful Balance. Every struggle and each story became a part of me. Your stories are the background for Beautiful Balance.

A big thank you to Margit Johns. Margit walked through leading and supporting me in the senior group at Juniper Village Meadville. The sweet seniors poured a vast amount of wisdom into Margit and me! Their aged wisdom on what loving God and loving others has looked like in their lives was a treasure trove of additions to the book!

To Diane and Connie, sisters of blood and heart. You never ran out of encouragement. You were there for every tear I cried and every stress I dumped on you. Sisters, this book is all about best friends and what real support can accomplish! Give it up for the girlfriends!

To Kristi, my friend and unbelievably best editor ever! I can't thank you enough for all the eye hours you poured into Beautiful Balance! Your love and generosity sent me to India once. I pray Beautiful Balance can love many Indian women into a brighter future!

To my co-workers at Meadville Middle school, thanks for your input on the back cover page. Your votes and suggestions made the cut!

To Joan Sommers, thank you for the last proof reading. And to Sheena Byham, thank you for the awesome photography that made me look so nice.

To my family, thank you for listening, being a sounding board for ideas and critiquing me when I asked for feedback. Thanks for all my undisturbed hours of typing in the dining room/BB office! I love you with all my heart and pray this book encourages you.

Blessings and may *Beautiful Balance* be yours!

Ellen

Beautiful Balance thanks you for journeying to joy!
Blessings as you become Beautifully Balanced
each day in loving God with your
whole spirit, mind, and body and loving others as yourself.

BEAUTIFUL BALANCE

Finding purpose in
God's two greatest
commandments.

"The most important one,"
answered Jesus,
"is this:
'Hear, O Israel:
The Lord our God,
the Lord is one.
Love the Lord your God
with all your heart and
with all your soul and
with all your mind
and with all your strength.'
The second is this:
'Love your neighbor as yourself.'
There is no commandment
greater than these."
Mark 12:29-31 NIV